STRANGE HOUSES OF SLEEP

BY

ARTHUR EDWARD WAITE

"Sciendum est igitur, dona omnia, in quibus vita nostra consistit, sacramentis et externis quibusdam sensibilibus signis tecta ac involuta esse."—SPECULUM DOMINI JOANNIS RUSBROCHII DIVINISSIMI CONTEMPLATORIS, Caput ix.

LONDON
PHILIP SINCLAIR WELLBY
MDCCCCVI

[illegible] Oxford Street, W. Hallett Hyatt Sc.

CONTENTS

PART I

SHADOWS OF SACRAMENTS

THE ARGUMENT

A. Ground Plans of the House of Life.—When a man begins to realise that he is normally in a dreaming state and that he must be aroused to attain himself, he is forthwith impelled to consider the mysteries of his sleep, the greater and lesser also, with the manifestations thereto belonging, and it is in this manner that he becomes dedicated to the interpretation of his dreams. Herein therefore is the general thesis of the dream-life, including certain vestiges, which are memories, of all that which is without it. It is in this way that a man awakens to the first sense of the quest. Being thus already in part illuminated, he puts in order his plans for the improvement of his symbolic position. He beholds indeed the first shining of the sacramental life, through which the rivers of sleep may become to him even as fountains of refreshment, and his environment as a Promise of May. There is torpor and there is inhibition, but there are also suggestions of states that have rewards beyond the dreams of avarice. A man is in effect already a Postulant at the Pronaos of the Temple.

B. Lesser Lights and Broideries of the Veil.—A man takes thought of Nature and her sacramental service, discovering after what manner some strange suspensions operate. Herein is the consideration in full of the palmary messages promulgated by the outside world. These are Watches of the Morning, wherein the insufficiency of Nature is made evident. A man has tried the normal ways and has not found satisfaction. Where are the Wings of Healing? Amid such preludes and pastorals of the world which leads to nothing ; in the realm of fragilities and the *Trivia;* he has met with certain mercies and judgments and has

Contents

Contents

Contents

Contents

Contents

Contents

Contents

Contents

PART II

THE HIDDEN SACRAMENT OF THE HOLY GRAAL

PART III

THE POOR BROTHER'S MASS-BOOK

Contents

Contents

Contents

PART IV

THE BOOK OF THE KING'S DOLE AND CHANTRY FOR PLAIN SONG: A GREATER INITIATION

THE ARGUMENT

Having been oft born in many initiations, a man takes the Exalting Veil and is received into the Heart of the Quest. This is a Hierophant and more than a Hierophant, for many Great Masters cannot witness his assumption. In this manner there comes to pass the desired awakening from dream, and the Wardens of the Watch-Towers of the World shall not tell after what manner the great sea shall in fine give up the secret.

PART I

SHADOWS OF SACRAMENTS

Strange Houses of Sleep

THE WORK OF OUR HANDS

HAUNTED by memories of his first abode,
Man, in the shadows of this earthly road,
Still vindicates the past his legends claim,
Home is for him the semblance of a name;
And yet with steadfastness—and frighten'd haste—
Something impels to build him in the waste
A temporary house of his own hands—
To overlook the melancholy lands
And all his shrouded, sad environment.
Wherefore, when first to grievous exile sent,
About his soul inhibited he wrought
A body fitted to the halting thought
Of those who slowly lapse toward troubled sleep,
Praying, if long, it may be also deep,
Yet counting scarcely on a true repose,
Since strife in place of peace their slumber knows.
And then, because such frame was frail and cold,
He built him many tenements to hold

STRANGE HOUSES OF SLEEP

His nakedness, lamenting in the gloom—
Tent, temple, palace and, in fine, the tomb:
But though the body, warm'd by hearth and bed,
Came through these makeshifts to be comforted,
His haunted soul, mourning the exile's fate,
Still cried aloud that it was desolate.

Thereafter houses of the mind he made—
The House of Love—and Death therein he laid;
The House of Faith—and there a foeman set
Those strange, sad cups which cause us to forget.
Devices also on the walls he wrote
Which when unwrit do nothingness denote
And nothing written. But the House of Pride
High did he raise, and therein magnified
The hopes and works beguiling his distress—
Yet this was void through very emptiness.
So passing thence to where some false lights shone,
He raised up Houses of Ambition,
But through the portals and the windows pour'd
The vacant faces of a spectral horde.
And the soul built with shame the House of Lust,
Where hands on walls write :—" Here is also
dust;"
And though strange voices crying: "Come away!"
Sound in the darkness, to this latest day
The transient buildings round about us rise.
One bond connects them in fantastic wise—
Houses of Sleep they are, to anxious dreams
Devoted—semblances of things and themes,

THE WORK OF OUR HANDS

Dim images derived from otherwhere.
Yea, this is also true: the House of Prayer
Is part and parcel of that mystic trance
Through which our Momus pageantries advance,
And no one wakes of all whom sense enrings.

Only the evidence of secret things
Bears witness in us of a kindling hour;
Through all strange seizures still it speaks with power,
And those most conscious of their sleeping state
Are haply drawing to the waking gate.
Peace on the Houses of their trance! Unfold,
Dawn, on their tarnish'd eyes, thy wells of gold!
And past all melancholy, clouded lands
Bring tidings of the House not built with hands.

STRANGE HOUSES OF SLEEP

ALTERNATION

I

THOU dost hear the ocean's tale
In the moonlight, very pale,
Since thy chamber opens wide
One great casement towards the tide.
But another window looks
Over marshes and their brooks;
And thy garden paths between
Brooks and window intervene:
When the evening breezes blow,
Hear me in these paths below!

II

Lest the great, insistent sea—
Day and night adjuring thee—
By the secret word it sings,
Take too far from human things;
For a little space apart
Hear the singing in my heart!
Or if things eternal make
So much music for thy sake,
Hearken, from thy seat above,
The still vaster deep of love!

FLIGHT

ONE REFUGE

WHEN our conventions' sad calamity
Shall after weary days our path permit
To issue undeterr'd and free,—
What then remains?
Forest and woodland world, the green,
Far sparkling plains?—
Or fair Romance to lead the lines of it
O'er azure seas serene?

FLIGHT

I SOOTHED a bird with a broken limb—
Why does a rose so sweetly smell?—
Bright were the eyes and the plumes of him;
O heart beat softer!—
Thou canst not tell.

Safe in a bower he was set to rest—
What is the secret of beauty's spell?—
He was woo'd to health in a lichen nest;
O sweet bird-singer!—
Thou canst not tell.

STRANGE HOUSES OF SLEEP

The bird flew out through a door ajar—
   Where flies the soul with the passing bell?—
High sounds his song at the evening star;
   O voice of freedom!—
                        Thou canst not tell.

Perchance why the rose has a scent so sweet—
   Where all white secrets of beauty dwell—
When the soul goes up from the dim retreat
   Through a door left open—
                        The soul shall tell.

THE SECOND SENSE

THE SECOND SENSE

Renew'd for ever are the lives of books
By every eye that in their pages looks;
And many are the meanings which they bear:
Like limpid depths of lakes and water-brooks,
To each who reads they show his image there.

NATURE and great books have their second sense,
In still cool wells, but few can charm it thence;
The purports deep by which the soul is stirr'd
Lurk not within the manifested word,
As many intimations dimly show,
Directing higher search to those who know.
Within ourselves the secret meaning lies,
And till we read it there with our own eyes
We miss those heights we dream of and grow lean
Through famish'd longing after things unseen—
Divined, not held.

We give that meaning shapes
Symbolic—in such signs the force escapes.
We take the letter of the Word; our wit,
In strange metathesis, we wear on it
And so all trace of any point expel.
We say the word is lost: but who shall tell?
For who has found? A few fond souls proclaim
Their mission to make known its scope and aim:

O vain assurance of the heart! As if
Earth's wise can speak, except in hieroglyph,
Or offer more than images! The deep
Gives these up; from still tarns of silence leap
Visions and voices, but the things discern'd
Are neither new nor those for which we yearn'd.
One testifies: "The dead in Him abide
And His forgiveness sets all wrath aside."
One whispers: "Sweet sleep!" One, with bended
head,
Says: "Tears of joy!" One: "Here is Living
Bread!"
And an absolving voice, with strength untold
Of pity and sweetness, breathes; "Be then
consoled!"
But underneath them all still flows the sea
Of the soul's unexpress'd immensity.

So leave it therefore, friends—with one last word
I also leave it thus: the sense unheard
Which lies for ever the bright veils behind
Of all the books of Nature and of Mind,
Eluding all approximating art,
Shall yield to—God known truly of the heart.
O did I start in mountain or abyss,
I could not choose but end at last in this!
From wayside taverns issuing should see
That this alone unlocks all mystery;
And rising fever'd out of beds of sin
Most truly feel it and to speak begin;

THE SECOND SENSE

Nor more in cloisters praying could recall
That this is end of end and all in all.
If things so many underneath the sun
Thus lead me ever to the arms of One,
Ye who do likewise strongly yearn, forgive—
Turn to this last again, and, turning, live.

So much, without distortion or offence,
A man may venture towards the second sense.
All pools Heaven rains in and all seas untrod
Go on reflecting heaven—beyond is God;
And 'twixt the gentleness of Nature's state
And the unsleeping heights, His people wait.

Great is the ministry of books, and great
Their consolation in our mean estate;
But hearts whose aches prolong with every beat,
Find them, like Nature's breathings, incomplete.

GREAT SILENCES

Ah, sighing grass! Ah, trees that know not rest!
All life of earth pressing to ends afar,
Heart's flight of man and hurry of every star—
What go ye forth to find? Where ends your quest?

STRANGE HOUSES OF SLEEP

CUPS THAT PASS IN THE NIGHT

Great were the taverns where we used to dwell,
Fired by strong cups which we could drain of yore;
The stories great which once we used to tell
And maxims now repeated never more;
Could any scribe have follow'd us—how great
Were truths we found in cups at early hours and late.

FIRST there was chaos, out of brooding bred—
Silent, inseparate, dispirited—
And yet with shapeless semblances impress'd—
Like one who drinks alone beside the dead,
Breast over breast !—

Who dipping deeply in a vintage rare,
Sees it is his own body lying there,
And, in confusion, calls on ghosts without
As boon companions in his watch to share—
A sorry rout.

So chaos moved, distracted in the night,
Conceiving horror of its depth and height,
Saw self in self reflect with deadly fear ;
Till that which cried above: Let there be Light !—
Made light appear.

CUPS THAT PASS IN THE NIGHT

Then all great forces strove its rays to reach—
As travellers at an inn the cups of each—
  And Tohu held with Bohu orgie high,
From which creation, full of silver speech,
  Sprang by and bye.

Then did the morning stars together sing,
As feasting princes who their glasses ring,
  And the great Bacchic chorus swell'd above;
Joy's shout was lifted upon rapture's wing,
  As wine lifts love.

And still creation holds that joy divine,
As the uplifted cup holds blood-red wine,
  And still the Cosmos, in its Mœnad dance,
From age to age, with eyes that brighter shine,
  Spins into trance.

We too are copies of the cosmic plan,
From earth's quintessence shaped to make us man,
  And that which Nature sketches in first place
We raise through purlieus out of bar and ban
  Towards gifts of grace.

Like chaos once, we dwelt, old friend, alone,
And drank with cold hearts foreign to our own,
  Or, in our solitude, perchance with none;
So to true life were dead as any stone
  Or corpse 'neath sun.

STRANGE HOUSES OF SLEEP

But now through purple hours of Bacchic night
We pass our cups, and in the depth and height
  Do each in each reflect with love, not fear ;
And when the heart within us cries for light
  Great lights appear.

We, like the morning stars, together sing,
What time in unison our glasses ring,
  With cosmic minds matured in vintage fine,
Exalting ever upon rapture's wing
  Æonian wine.

And as creation, on some purpose bent,
Moves grandly forward, fill'd with high content,
  We, slowly down the road of years withdrawn,
Note from each tavern where the night is spent
  Each breaking dawn.

O world, created in a vintage song,
We know thy goal is good, though ways be long !
  Strange cups pass too among the stars en-
      crown'd—
The ecstasy is great, the wine is strong,
  WHAT GRAALS ARE FOUND !

THE SCARLET SWAN

THE SCARLET SWAN

HERE is high teaching from the far blue lift,
For Madeline, sweet maid of Mary's gift,
By certain stars transmitted on a beam
   Of argent splendour through a lilac haze;
A legend of the land which is not dream
   Or waking, as of eyes in earthly ways,
Under the crimson splendours of the morn,
But something greater which from both is born
And far o'er life abides, in joyful stress,
Full of high state and thoughtful solemness.

Now list! That Madeline of white and red
Rose blooms was wrought, who doubts? The wise
      have said—
   And the gold hair, assuredly, of her
Shone once upon the King-Sun's royal head,
   As all the elfin parables aver,
Whence sunshine loves so well to brood thereon;
But all of scarlet was the Flying Swan
Which, on the day that Madeline was made,
God in such glory of bright plumes array'd,
And so commission'd over starry tides
Saying:—Dear heart, have courage, a rest abides!

STRANGE HOUSES OF SLEEP

Now thus it is that through the breathless deeps
Of heaven's great space upon his flight he keeps:
Star after star upon the Scarlet Swan,
Pours floods of light, and ever and anon,
Athwart his path, the comets with a crash
Hurtle, the falling meteors seethe and flash;
Dark worlds, bereft of all the fire within,
Blind in the void about him feebly spin;
And where in luminous mists the starry seeds
Show myriad points of light, swift-wing'd, he
speeds.

Must he not weary? For deep rest indeed
Longs he not, dreaming of the waters cool,
The clear brown stillness of some shaded pool,
A nest engirded by a world of reed?
I know at least, with keen eyes fix'd before,
And fill'd with frighten'd longing, evermore
He labours night and day to reach his end;
On Madeline, of Mary's gift, alone,
As legends tell, for help his wings depend,
Lest he faint somewhere on his paths unknown.

The Scarlet Swan to Mary's gift is bound;
With her it rests that he shall reach his end:
If she on earth is full of goodness found,
Strength and high purpose to his heart ascend.
When Mary's gift aspires to Mary's throne,
And with the will of heaven unites her own,

THE SCARLET SWAN

Asleep on dreaming wings he softly glides
And towards his end is drawn by silent tides;
But when from maiden grace and fair estate
She stoops awhile, sad is the wanderer's fate;
His flagging wings athwart the stir and stress
Of hostile currents wildly forward press;
Against dark worlds he strikes, and stars that fall
With desolating shrieks his heart appal—
Alone, St. Mary's gift; what weariness!

Now, therefore, Madeline shall, inly stirr'd,
By this most faithful legend's secret word,
Reflect for ever in her heart thereon,
That so all grace and strength the Scarlet Swan
Shall visit in his flight, and sleep be his,
With winds that favour, till he reach where is—
O joy!—the refuge of a restful town.
Then, Swan no more, Bright Spirit under crown,
After such struggles, shall God applaud the pains,
Saying:—Dear heart, be welcome; rest remains!

Stars, and a thousand stars, and lilac lift—
God save the Scarlet Swan, save Mary's gift!

STRANGE HOUSES OF SLEEP

THEY THAT WORK IN SILENCE

A SPACE of sleep vouchsafe the Lords of love;
To wake at length they grant who reign above;
  And many substitutes for rest high schemes
Dispense, till pity their great hearts shall move
  To free us from our dreams.

They that have rock'd us into swoon so well
Alone can break the bars and bonds of spell;
  But surely comes the wakening at last,
When each to each of all his toils shall tell
  As of old dangers past.

And towards the place of exile, far away,
We shall look back in our relief and say:
  Hard was the bed whereon we writhed in sleep;
But now the vigils of true life repay
  With rest divinely deep.

THE HEIGHTS REMAIN

THE HEIGHTS REMAIN

WE saw thee drop this day in circles down,
Dear lark, into thy nest! The stream is brown,
With silver streak'd; upon the left it glows,
Made broad by summer floods. The south wind
blows,
The road is white in front, and blue thou art,
O summer sky! Thy beauty takes the heart.
What gleams high up on yonder distant hill,
This moment brought in view? The white road still!
Great soul, to stand upon that soaring peak
And feel the wind of heaven on either cheek!
But at the base three several tracks divide,
And that which we must take turns there aside;
Wide uplands slope upon the left and right,
The trees grow thicker towards the airy height
Freshens the wind advancing. We shall pass
A furlong's space over the light lawn grass;
The quickset hedge will part, the path will take
Our steps a little into bower and brake,
Then into forest shade and mystery.
So, if we miss the heights we yet shall see
What revelations may, in glades conceal'd
And sudden clearings, be to eye reveal'd;

STRANGE HOUSES OF SLEEP

What shapes of beauty down green vistas wait
And who sings sweetly at the farmyard gate;
Or, when those distant bells' sweet jangles cease,
Feel what it is which gives the woodland peace,
And why the spring, which keeps so still through noon,
Begins towards eve to chatter for the moon;
Till, after winding for a mile or less,
The path comes gaily from the wilderness
And gives us back once more to wind and sky.
There, over pleasant meadows, soaring high
The peak again invites the climber's feet.
So we who have explored the green retreat
And something of its lesser secrets learn'd,
Lose nothing from our course a moment turn'd,
Since the exulting heights still rest to climb—
To-day, to-morrow, or in after time.

OF TRUE AND FALSE MARRIAGES

OF TRUE AND FALSE MARRIAGES

Earth has its nuptials and the flesh shall know
What flesh can learn of unions here below;
But the soul coming from some far-off place,
Hath look'd not yet upon the bridegroom's face,
And therefore goeth sadly here along.
Give up, O void of voids, the marriage song!
Above earth's jarring measures and their noise,
Call us in peace unto the nuptial joys.

"Whom God hath join'd"—aye, that leaves room for wonder,
Granting — who doubts? — that none can put asunder:
But seeing that two lovers in one bed
Are further each from each,
As Love itself will teach,
Than any star is far from them o'er head,
This question still recurs:
Whom hath God join'd?

Think you, his flesh to hers
By stratagem, from other arms purloin'd,
And she not surely first, nor he the last
While simple passion is so quickly past

Or courts remain to utter their decrees?
But think you any marriage of the flesh?
True, they shall part not when their earth is dead
Who, few and rarely, in their souls are wed.
Past doubt, eternity, assuming these,
Transfigures the old bonds or welds afresh;
But their true souls how few on earth have found,
Much less with others have their own been bound,
And skin-deep wedlock with the joys it brings
Scarce counts among indissoluble things.

Alas, the things which once God join'd, through some
Deep-seated mischief, to divorce have come;
And it is only when the lights within
From height exceeding height some lustre win—
Cold, inaccessible and clear—
The space-immensities of winter's clime—
Or great distractions fallen on the sea,
Beyond all deeps of time—
That pasts withdrawn in worlds of memory
Send faint reports—though bands of sense enfold—
Of great free unions which obtain'd of old.

Naked we are, divorced from our true ends,
And conscious only of what pain attends
The isolation on our course imposed,
The hush of prospects from all points disclosed;

OF TRUE AND FALSE MARRIAGES

Yea, on the nuptial night man stands alone
And lonely walks the wife he calls his own:
  Veil'd limbs and shrouded lips—
Of such are our most close companionships,
Sad travesty of joys that once we knew.
Pass as we can this mournful exile through,
But ask not constancy and faith too much;
Of loving kindness seek the healing touch,
And let us deal with those who share our lot
As if all mercy were, all judgment not;
Keep, if we may, through this life's stormy weather,
But say not rashly God hath join'd together.
What did God join? Man to the star he seeks,
Sea to the soul to which the sea-deep speaks.
Off with these bonds! Over the great abyss
The far-off hope proclaims what union is,
And all that cannot rest in man's vast deep
Till it returns to God and there finds sleep
Has since creation in our inmost cried:
What God hath join'd who was it dared divide?

THE POET SPEAKS

WITH silent steps thou movest, Moon, on high,
For ever keeping thine appointed course!
What hope of rest is thine? What native source
Dost thou for peace seek out? The days go by—
There comes no end in sight, no haven nigh:
What impulse prompts thee on thy starry road?
Ah, shine! Thy roamings bless this dark abode;
With mild effulgence fill the ample sky.
O Solitary Lady, we have grown—
Our eyes so long on thy long journey fix'd—
Almost content to be, like thee, alone,
In steadfast thought, with other thought unmix'd;
Our paths, like thine, go upward and descend;
Aside we cannot swerve, or see the end.

THE LIGHTER VEIN

READY pen and easy thought,
   Turning out a lilting verse;
Here a flash of fancy caught,
There an artful image wrought—
   Could be better, might be worse!

Easy comes and easy goes
   The too light, fantastic rhyme—
Tinkles, twitters, sparkles, flows;
Nothing matters, no one knows;
   Who shall care in after time?

Saving grace or pleasing wit
   Jingling for the hour it can—
Something miss'd and something hit—
He that runs may read in it,
   Vex not thou its transient plan!

Leave it—organ songs of old
   Peal from out the ages gone;
Other times shall yet behold
Singers come with mouths of gold;
   Till then let it babble on.

HEMLOCK

You know that, in the last resource of all,
It matters scarcely how the light may fall,
Or what stars in the night their beacons lift.
So little also brings the morning's gift
That whether late or early Nature stir,
We mark but idly how it fares with her
When in the East the scarlet glories spill,
Or how at noon her children take their fill
Of all the good which warmth and brightness bring.
Who counts this other than a trivial thing,
Having so much, unmurmuring, left behind
Of all the morning splendours of the mind
And all life's midway majesty and pride?
One great detachment puts the soul aside
From the fair outward fields which Nature owns,
Since some time sadly seeking certain thrones,
Remember'd ever through a world of wrong,
The soul went forth. She, having journey'd long
Amidst the sorrows of secluded tracts,
Among cold snows and frozen cataracts,
Above the common zones of human thought,
One burden of sad knowledge thence has brought:—
That in such altitudes all stars look thin.
So, 'twixt the throne you surely thought to win

And that last dizzy peak of precipice
Where you have dared to stand, the great abyss
Its void unfathom'd offers silently.

Now, hence it is that though the eye may see,
With sight herein it is not satisfied,
Nor is the ear by hearing occupied,
And nothing ministers of all things round.
For as the man who looking to be crown'd
Amidst high pageantry at eve, if left
Outside the palace, of all state bereft,
Would little comfort find that Western skies
Show over wide meads phantom pageantries,
And though the stars may shine in all their state
Would still keep knocking at the Palace Gate;
So, dedicated unto larger things
Than all experiments of earthly kings,
And having strongly striven to ascend
Where great gods are, but having miss'd our end,
By reason of the gulfs which intervene:
What wonder now that all this earthly scene
Spectral and pallid to the soul appear?

Yet this is desolation; hemlock here
We drink henceforth through all the aching void,
Taking the cross of our fair hope destroy'd,
No longer with the scheme of things in touch.
But, lest our mingled cup should over-much
Embitter us, and those whom thought intense
Has worn, seem ravaged by the work of sense,

STRANGE HOUSES OF SLEEP

Like any worldling underneath the sun—
We still remember that which once was done,
When, some time sadly seeking certain thrones,
Beyond the outward fields which Nature owns,
On that last dizzy peak of precipice
We were held only by the great abyss;
And when we most may turn from mortal things
It is in longing for unearthly wings,
Or at the utmost solitary ridge
Still in the end to find a secret bridge.

AT THE END OF THINGS

THE world uprose as a man to find Him—
  Ten thousand methods, ten thousand ends—
Some bent on treasure; the more on pleasure;
  And some on the chaplet which fame attends:
But the great deep's voice in the distance dim
Said: Peace, it is well; they are seeking Him.

When I heard that all the world was questing,
  I look'd for a palmer's staff and found,
By a reed-fringed pond, a fork'd hazel-wand
  On a twisted tree, in a bann'd waste ground;
But I knew not then what the sounding strings
Of the sea harps say at the end of things.

AT THE END OF THINGS

They told me, world, you were keen on seeking;
I cast around for a scrip to hold
Such meagre needs as the roots of weeds—
All weeds, but one with a root of gold;
Yet I knew not then how the clangs ascend
When the sea-horns peal and the searchings end.

An old worn wallet was that they gave me,
With twelve old signs on its seven old skins;
And a star I stole for the good of my soul,
Lest the darkness came down on my sins;
For I knew not who in their life had heard
Of the sea-pipes shrilling a secret word.

I join'd the quest that the world was making,
Which follow'd the false ways far and wide,
While a thousand cheats in the lanes and streets
Offer'd that wavering crowd to guide;
But what did they know of the sea-reed's speech
When the peace-words breathe at the end for each?

The fools fell down in the swamps and marshes;
The fools died hard on the crags and hills;
The lies which cheated, so long repeated,
Deceived, in spite of their evil wills,
Those knaves themselves at the end of all—
Though how should they hearken when sea-flutes call?

But me the scrip and the staff had strengthen'd;
  I carried the star; that star led me:
The paths I've taken, of most forsaken,
  Do surely lead to the open sea:
As a clamour of voices heard in sleep,
Come shouts through the dark on the shrouded deep.

Now it is noon; in the hush prevailing
  Pipes, harps and horns into flute-notes fall;
The sea, conceding my star's true leading,
  In tongues sublime at the end of all
Gives resonant utterance far and near:—
            "Cast away fear;
             Be of good cheer;
             He is here,
               Is here!"

And now I know that I sought Him only
  Even as child, when for flowers I sought;
In the sins of youth, as in search for truth,
  To find Him, hold Him alone I wrought.
The knaves too desire Him, and fools beguiled—
So speak to them also, sea-voices mild!

Which then was wisdom and which was folly?
  Did my star more than the cozening guide?
The fool, as I think, at the chasm's brink,
  Prone by the swamp or the marsh's side,
Did, even as I, in the end rejoice,
Since the voice of death must be needs His voice.

A BRIDGE FROM EARTH

A BRIDGE FROM EARTH

Away with time-worn thought! Who gives free space
Of seemly silence, in some form of tongue
Not wholly secret, not at least unknown,
May hear God speak, and shall that speech to men,
His brothers, by the haste of eager days
Distracted, in due season and in part
Interpret. A fair world before me now
Spreads, past indeed most bounds of daily walk,
But yet not more than commonly removed,
And, strong and sweet, God's speech goes over it
In winds which freshen ; in the bright, blue sky—
The high, clear sky swept bright by Autumn winds—
His eyes are shining. What if in the South
The dark clouds roll, and gather'd in the West
Below their bank, of black, foreboding mien,
Far droop long tendrils down of angry light?
These hold some other mystery of God
Behind them, and a pearl is in the mist
On certain fields before me. At my feet,
O'er all this down, the heath's dark green and rich
Begins to burst with blossom. Now it breaks—
Yes, breaks the sunshine forth ; all heaven looks out,
Earth strips all shades to greet me. Like a voice,

STRANGE HOUSES OF SLEEP

The beauty round me calls on every side,
"Awake! Arise!" And broad on farther slopes
The road ascends, while all the loose brown earth
Of fields fresh plough'd deep glows with amber hues.
Fair sleeps the vale between us—pastures rich,
Dark gold of woods. Speech in the winds indeed—
Eyes in the light; but in the still life too
An eloquence of silence, in the holds
Of solemn shadow such a frequent hint
Of high intelligence, on secret things
So wisely brooding; at our doors, our hands,
On every side the earth puts forth a bridge,
Or lifts a ladder, or a path makes smooth
From less to great till earth of all the worlds
Is nighest thing to heaven and stars to man.

AT THAT DOOR

In the late night—full sorrowful and cold,
  I stood by mine own door and knock'd;
White mists against the vacant windows roll'd;
  The house was barr'd and lock'd.

The house was lock'd, and desolate and void,
  The forecourt wild and damp without;
The rose was scatter'd and the vine destroy'd;
  Loose tiles were strewn about.

AT THAT DOOR

From ragged eaves the stealthy moisture dripp'd;
  The moss upon the steps was green;
The foot along the reedy pathways slipp'd
  On fungus growths unclean.

No link was set within the time-worn sconce,
  No lamp in porch to show the way;
Cypress and yew made ominous response
  To wind more sad than they.

No loving hand was there to let me in,
  No voice behind the portal spoke,
But at the knocker's unaccustom'd din
  The passage echoes woke.

And yet meseem'd I went forth yester morn
  From warmth and light and peace within;
Whence, if I tarried in that place forlorn,
  Eftsoons must day begin.

But still for ever, in the vapour's shroud,
  The moon leans sideways from the sky,
And in the dark east speaks no saffron cloud
  Of morrow's morning nigh.

Ah, what distress! Of mine own house denied,
  Acold beside its portals dumb
And vacant windows staring blind and wide,
  That dawn will never come.

STRANGE HOUSES OF SLEEP

TAKING THE VEIL

"*L'esprit se revête pour descendre et se dépouille pour monter.*"

Folds of flesh henceforth enwind thee,
 Earthly veils thy form conceal,
Five restricted senses bind thee—
 Dimly wails our vain appeal.

Wings of those that loved and knew thee
 Round about thy house may throng,
But the charm of life which drew thee
 Holds thee by a spell too strong.

Soul of sweetness, thus forsaking
 True life's light and love divine,
When the witch-spell fails, awaking—
 Light and life and love be thine.

So the walls of earth entomb thee,
 So we leave thee—born of men;
May thy sisters' hands assume thee
 Born in death to life again.

ILLUMINATION

ILLUMINATION

I

WITH native ease the serpent sloughs his skin,
But cannot change his old snake-heart within;
Man does not lay his outward form aside,
Yet can his old life from his new divide.

II

The simple words which follow shall direct
Right well and pleasantly all hearts elect,
And little children of the world to come;
But unto others be in meaning dumb—
Vague voices which delight on stormy seas
In unintelligible images:
May all who read these maxims sweetly reach
Late, if not soon—the truths exceeding speech!

III

What makes us say that underneath the sun
The toil we call our own is toil undone—
Finds work, when others sleep, for hand and heart
And from repose shapes obstacles to art?

It is the sense of trust which burdens thought:
In these wild ways ungovern'd and untaught
We came some solemn purpose to fulfil,
And till encompass'd in its whole extent
We cannot say that we indeed were sent,
Nor yet be sure we do the Master's will.

IV

Something has gone before us in the past,
And something more must follow at the last.

V

Man enters life expectant, and departs
With expectation in his heart of hearts.

VI

He dwelt in darkness ere his birth occurr'd
And oft in darkness still his strife is heard,
Toiling a higher title to attain;
His throes are those of being born again.

VII

The universe he enters here bestows
Such earthly lights on him as Nature knows,
And sustenance is his from brimming wells
Of its white sacraments and parables;

Through all its veils the presages are brought
Of greater orders—passing human thought—
Which interpenetrate at times our own:
In Grace and Nature nothing stands alone.

VIII

When souls come down into this world they take
The letter of the books, their thirst to slake;
The spirit in the Temple's place conferr'd
Is in the inmost Temple only heard;
And that which darkness doth from dawn divide
Renders it always night, the soul outside.

IX

As every witness in the heart avers,
No dispensation of the light occurs,
Save in that shrine which earth's eye never sees,
The place withdrawn of the Great Mysteries.
Subject and object there Plotinus found
United truly on a common ground.
What place is that? Ye neophytes—it lurks
Deep in the heart of these external works!

X

High rites in all their stages can dispense
Only the sanctuary's secret sense,
And can at most in empty hearts arouse
The hunger for the beauty of the House.

XI

Now, last, remember that which none deny—
Clean life leads no man into sanctity,
And hence no mere morality can gain
That vision which the pure in heart attain.

XII

But what is raised, magnetically draws
All things to reach it; this is law of laws.

XIII

A golden ring unites such scatter'd Keys,
Which open portals to the Mysteries.

A DIRGE AT SEA

Well hast thou chosen who hast made the sea
Thy resting place! O, all things bright and high
Claim kinship with it! By the ample moon
'Tis drawn for ever, and in turn the sea
Draws all great souls; it is the soul of earth.
Bereft thereof the stony coasts would stretch
As dead and barren as the wilted moon,
Which has no life but that which dwells in dread
Desire of soul, which vainly strives to steal,
O earth, thy soul away!

A DIRGE AT SEA

Sleep, gentle flesh!
The cool sea water takes thee: in its blue
Thine eyes henceforth shall glisten; there thy lips
Shall tinge its groves of coral; all the white
And delicate flesh dissolving shall become
A portion of its being. So the thought—
The sacred thought of thee—shall still keep fresh
That calm, vast heart.

The mermaids draw thee down,
To deep sea temples, there with mystic rites
Perform thine obsequies. To its true home
The flesh returns, thy spirit to its place
Is render'd too; throughout all days to come
That soul to mine inseparably join'd,
With light and beauty, like a sacrament,
Shall all my nature penetrate and change.

STRANGE HOUSES OF SLEEP

A DREAM OF JUNE

THE splendid pageantry of sunset takes
  The dreamer forth along the winding road,
What time the dewdrop in the roses makes,
  Descending silently, its night abode ;
What time the hedge-rose lifts a coral cup,
About the dew's cool treasure closing up.
    Now sunset roses o'er the wintry way
    Alone recall the rose of yesterday.

With fragile petals delicate of hue—
  The sweetest flower that in the country blooms—
The wayside rose, 'neath heaven's imperial blue,
  Dispenses its felicitous perfumes,
While dying daylight's gold and scarlet flood
With sudden glory tinges leaf and bud.
    The snow-drift quenches now the dying beam ;
    The rose of sunset is itself a dream.

O floral chalice, on the hedge so high,
  May gentle rains, that soothe the thirsty land,
Refresh thy blossom from a gracious sky !
  May thorns for ever from the rustic hand

A DREAM OF JUNE

Thine elfin beauties jealously defend,
And thy last petal to its latest end!
May dark December's bleak and dreary stress
Be soothed with memories of thy loveliness!

May temper'd winds about thy spaces green
Breathe light in modulated music low!
May golden bees, when thy full bloom is seen,
Extract its mellow sweets to overflow
The deep recesses of their tree-built homes,
And fill with winter stores their honeycombs!
And in man's image-haunted hives of thought
Not all in vain may thy June sweets be sought!

Those fairy children, born of summer's bliss,
The moths that flit through fruitful fields beyond,
With wings of azure, where thy beauty is
For ever hover in a silence fond!
And with deep rapture, all the day long ringing,
May thy fair world ne'er want a lark's blithe singing!
The leaves of thought which thy sere petals hold
Shall echoes also of that song enfold.

O may thy fabled love, the nightingale,
Through all night's calm and visionary space,
In glow-worm haunted thicket, or deep vale,
Abide at hand, musician of thy grace;
And all the senses of thy floral soul
With rapture ravish, with delight control!
Soft falls the snow from leaden lift above;
Soft in our hearts repose, O flower of love!

STRANGE HOUSES OF SLEEP

The poet's benediction dowers thee well—
  Was that thy blush upon the western sky?
Was that thy beauty over field and fell
  Investing all in gorgeous panoply?
Ah, when deep night envelopes all things here,
Thy fragrance still proclaims that thou art near!
    Still art thou with us under Christmas snows,
    For us the rose ne'er dies—long live the rose!

The Rose and Rose, for evermore the Rose,
  While days are dwindling towards the least of all
And every utterance sadly sets towards close;
  The shadow of life itself has ceased to fall;
Ferment and sap of life no longer work;
All the quick light is still'd in shroud of murk:
    Yet it is daylight shortly, torrid sun;
    A thousand Roses in the place of one!

A GREY WORLD

A GREY WORLD

The horse is warm in his stall,
Warm in his hut lies the thrall;
A measured music, grand and dim,
Heard from afar, is the angels' hymn:
Turn horse in stall and churl on bed;
Angels of Issa, bend the head:
Let all waif-children be comforted!

THESE things in a vision saw I,
But they rest with me till I die,
And ever the pity grows in my heart
For all earth's stray'd ones, her counterpart.

Now, the child was striving where great downs rose,
And about the downs the hills did close;
Peak above peak, with a frozen crown,
Each mountain over the hills look'd down:
The sky was snow and within it all
Was a sense of night which could not fall,
While the wind, which seem'd to carry a cross,
Scream'd the eternal sense of loss:
Yet through that wailing world of grey
The pale waif follow'd her woful way.

STRANGE HOUSES OF SLEEP

The child was wretched, the child was bare,
And, for greater horror, was lonely there;
No single face in that stricken zone
Had bent in kindness to meet her own,
Or offer'd the grasp of a helping hand,
For no man dwelt in the dreadful land,
And the tender heart of a woman had not
For ever lighten'd her orphan lot.
It seem'd that since the beginning of things
Such feet came less than an angel's wings,
And the kind sweet angels, it is known,
Only encircle a great white throne,
Or if below them they turn their faces,
'Tis not to gaze on accursèd places.

She went on trying some goal to reach,
As a lost child strives who has none to teach;
But she knew not whence she had come, nor
    whither
Tended the path which had brought her thither,
And fear—which is worse than a frozen track
Through an ice-world stretching at front and
    back—
Forbade the pulses of thought to stir
And wither'd the poor little heart of her:
One thing only, by waste and hill
Something drove her to hasten still,
Lest cross more dreadful and greater woes
In that world's unrest should befall repose.

A GREY WORLD

Over the waste, through the mist so wan,
The tortuous path went on and on—
What purpose serving exceeded wit:
Say, is there light at the end of it?
And after all, in the scheme of things,
Is the child protected by unseen wings?
Or is this only a show which seems?—
Shall the waif wake up from uneasy dreams
On a bed of down, where bright rays are falling,
To hear the voice of her mother calling,
Saying: "Sweet maid, it is late, so late,
And out in the garden your sisters wait
In the morning shine, while the bells begin
To usher my dear one's birthday in?"

The grey clouds gather from rim to lift
And the child enters a great snow drift;
The sharp flakes stifle her wailing cry,
The peaks are lost in a blank of sky;
If God is behind this doom and wrath,
She will haply issue on smoother path,
But I know not, granting all crowns of bliss,
For what good end it is ruled like this,

While the horse is warm in his stall,
And warm in his hut lies the thrall;
And a high chant filling the heavens says thus:—
"But Thou, O Lord, have mercy on us!"
Angels of Issa, bow the head,
Till all waif-children are comforted.

STRANGE HOUSES OF SLEEP

WHITHER?

THE moon does not tire in the sky,
Nor the star which comes after it quail
In the paths that are high;
But they know where they go,
While we faint and we fail,
For we know not, ah, no!
Sure light, that has lighted from time out of mind,
As we look from our place,
Still we dream by such grace
We may find!

DISTRACTION

SHALL a poet whose office is high
For the heights, say, a moment unapt,
Descend some distraction to try
And adapt?

The thought in itself gives a touch
Of the trivial to help his descent:
Will such deeps be more deep overmuch
Than he meant?

DISTRACTION

'Tis assumed he must cleave to his part
   But may seek with conventions to toy,
See if flowers of the field will his heart
      Offer joy:

If the pastoral landscapes can please,
   And Phyllis becoming will seem
When the pipes of a Colin give ease
      In his dream.

There's not much in this, as we know;
   Shall he turn with an amorous gaze,
Of a courtlier mistress or so
      Singing praise?

Shall he find in his country a theme,
   Or the party he follows advance?
Shall he give some benevolent scheme
      A rhyme's chance?

We may doubt if distraction in these
   Can be won from his call overlong,
Or that ways which are beaten will please
      For his song.

For the things which are done may be done,
   It is true, in a different way;
But the woof which is spun has been spun,
      Well aday!

STRANGE HOUSES OF SLEEP

And the ends which are far out of reach,
Green earth and the sky that is blue
Exceeding, please most for our speech
Me and you.

Leave, therefore, the lambs to their fold
And the sheep to the shepherds who tend,
Since the themes which are old will be old
To the end.

But above one and all are the peak's
Revelations, for song that can dare,
In pursuit of the high things it seeks,
To go there.

IMMANENCE

THE wind without is wild on down and cliff
But here is perfect shelter. Pause with me
By this rude stile; and, past the mellow browns
Of autumn bushes on the broken slopes,
Behold the sea below, the vault above,
The mist's thin draperies, the ghost—scarce seen—
Of yon young moon suspended white and thin!

IMMANENCE

I count it good to stand, as now we stand,
This resonant September afternoon,
And, past the twisted shapes of oak and beech,
To see the low, slow, sounding waves far down—
Churn'd on the rocks and stain'd by yellow sand—
Advance incessantly. The air is cool;
Here wanes the day; from this glen's marshy slope
Comes subtle fragrance; and that shelving bank,
Where oaks still hold against the stir and stress
Their sering leaves, alone from sight shuts out
A blazing autumn sunset's scene sublime.

The coastguard's cottage windows facing West
Are flaming strangely. Now the night descends—
Alas, the turf looks cold, forlorn and grey!
Our steps retrace! Once more the hill we climb—
Green, orange, crimson—is the world ablaze?
Is the sea burning? Are those loose black clouds,
Which, with the wind, pass off from North to East,
The smoke thereof? It is the sunset—see!
Confess the Presence—watch, but speak no more!

STRANGE HOUSES OF SLEEP

A FREE WAY

THE green hedge grows by the dull wayside,
And for no sweet reason or artful sense,
But merely a landmark, rises a fence,
  And a gate in the fence stands wide.
Close—on the further side of the hedge—
To the ditch's brink is the oozy edge
  Of a shoal and torpid pond.
A random foot-way falters beyond,
  Its narrow track in the woodland screening.
The hedge is ragged, the shoots spring high;
Through gaps and breaches you see the sky,
But I doubt if even a dreamer's eye
  Could clothe it with secret meaning:
Nor seems that twig, from the rest up-rising
Twelve inches straight in the air or more,
A guide-post stretch'd to an unknown shore
  For a good stout heart's emprizing.
Yet on certain nights—when the moon is late—
In front of the moon's disc, dark and straight,
With a single leaf will the twig stand clear,
  Moved by the night-wind's hand unseen;
And a still small voice in the dreamer's ear
  Begins to murmur and keen.
Very softly there, very sadly here,

A NIGHT PIECE

Sway'd South or North by the viewless hand,
The leaf says: "Here it is Fairyland!"
  And then, more plainly:
"He that looks further is searching vainly:
  Near, near—never so near:
The gate is open, the path is free;
It is now, if ever, to hear and see!"
And I see for one—through this message coming
In the midst of the dusk night's drowsy humming—
That to him who can hear and understand
Why this is the entrance of Fairyland,
May even a twig and a leaf impart
Some secrets hidden in Nature's heart.
Whence I conclude that the end of things
Exceeds not the sweep of an angel's wings,
And if these spread widely from base to marge,
We know He has given His angels charge.

A NIGHT PIECE

On the drench'd sands and shallow windless sea,
On that one boat which rocks, with one bare mast,
At anchor, on a hundred naked groynes,
And on the desolate and sinking house,
With crumbling turrets facing towards the tide,
There falls, like stillness on the close of Time—
A soft and mournful mist—the sad, grey night.

STRANGE HOUSES OF SLEEP

SEASONS

FOR ever the autumn and spring
And for ever on shining wing,
A Summer which goes and returns ;
But oh for the cleansing fount,
Dear heart, of the Holy Mount,
For which ever the true heart yearns !

OF SLEEPING AND WAKING

THAT virgin peer who sought the Holy Graal
Found in the castle hall his senses fail,
By heavy slumber strangely overweigh'd.
The pomp, through smoke of censers slowly sway'd,
Swept by him, prone with limbs that never stirr'd
And lips that moved not with the questing word,
Which would the hidden mystery reveal
And the King's hurts and all the country heal.
Therefrom the woe wax'd greater more and more.
So also we, who our sad state deplore,

BENISONS

Of hidden oracle and holy lips
Ask secret lights, the passwords and the grips;
But when the vision from the veil replies
Sleep falls full heavy on our souls and eyes,
And whether it is spoken or withheld
It utters nothing to our senses spell'd.
O Knight of Arthur's court, after great stress
You saw the hallows which could heal and bless:
May we in time our long enchantment break
And to the word of life from sleep awake!

BENISONS

BLEST be this undergrowth! May rain and dew
Increase it still! And blest the tranquil breeze
Which after cooling showers has crept across
From dark, rich downs that ring the country round
Blest too this sky of June, like April's seen—
Glory of sapphire blue, glory of cloud!

STRANGE HOUSES OF SLEEP

SUSPIRIUM

Where art thou ?—Where ?—Speak to me once—
divide
The dreadful hush of death ! Cold grave and dark,
Didst thou hold anything of her I loved,
This adjuration and this agony
Should vitalise the remnants into life—
So should I hear of thee ! Thou dost not sleep ;
Drawn through high portals of eternity
Thou art awake, abroad : but where art thou ?
Give me a sign upon the sky to know—
Or let thy tears fall, light as softest down
From dreaming swan upon a pool's still breast,
O'er mine uplifted face, if tears be thine.

Oh lady, thou didst once, a moon at night,
Shine burnish'd with a pale and psychic grace,
An argent beauty, toned and soften'd down
From all hard outlines of reality
Into a face of dream, which melted all
And the waste world about thee fill'd with love,
As thy sweet magic fill'd the sphere of life !
But after, stricken in a woeful time—
As sometimes night, star-panoplied, supreme

SUSPIRIUM

And saturate with artemisian light,
Grows wan before a vague and dreary day,
And earth's moon, dying in the white distraught
Turns to a pallid shadow—thou didst wane;
And hence the mercy of all-patient God
Was written in agony through all my youth,
But thou wast martyr'd more who now art crown'd.
So for thy sufferings' sake, my love, my loss
And the long dereliction of my days,
I swore to wear thenceforth a life unstain'd,
That none should suffer who environ'd me;
So did a heart of pity and pure love
With generous pulses fill the chords of life
And there is none that I have wrong'd—not one.

Therefore, I pray thee, let this exile end;
In thy clean hands the spirit I have kept
Pure for thy sake, I place. Let the still air
Give up the soft light of thine eyes; and come—
Come in thy mildness; or, that boon denied,
Strong in my yearning, bid me go to thee!

STRANGE HOUSES OF SLEEP

A LADDER OF LIFE

From age to age in the public place,
With the under steps in view,
The stairway stands, having earth for base,
But the heavens it passes through.

Height and deep,
And a dream for sleep,
Yet the Word of the King says well,
That the heart of the King is unsearchable.

Of the upmost steps there are legends grand,
Where the far stars shine as they roll;
But of child or man in the wonderful land
There is none who has scaled the whole.

And the great hope stirs,
Though His thoughts as yours
Are not, since the first man fell;
For the heart of the King is unsearchable.

A pulsing song of the stairway strange
Sing, lark, dissolved in the sky!
But no, for it passes beyond the range
Of thy song and thy soaring high.

The star is kin
To our soul within—
God orders His world so well:
Yet the heart of the King is unsearchable.

A LADDER OF LIFE

They say that the angels thereby came down,
  Thereby do the saints ascend,
And that God's light shining from God's own
    Town
  May be seen at the stairway's end.

    For good and ill
    May be mixed at will,
    The false show true by a spell,
    But the heart of the King is unsearchable.

Now the stairway stands by the noisy mart
  And the stairway stands by the sea;
About it pulses the world's great heart
  And the heart of yourself and me.

    We may read amiss
    Both in that and this,
    And the truth we read in a well;
    Since the heart of the King is unsearchable.

For a few steps here and a few steps there
  It is fill'd with our voices loud,
But above these slumbers the silent air
  And the hush of the dreaming cloud.

    In the strain and stress
    Of that silentness,
    The heart for the height may swell;
    But the heart of the King is unsearchable.

STRANGE HOUSES OF SLEEP

Now, some of us fill'd with a holy fire
The Cross and the Christ have kiss'd;
We have sworn to achieve our soul's desire
On book and evangelist:

Of step the third
I can bring down word,
And you on the fifth may dwell;
Yet the heart of the King is unsearchable.

As each of us stands at his place assign'd
And dreams of the things we love,
It is meet and right we should call to mind
That some must have pass'd above:

Yes, some there are
Who have passed so far,
They have never return'd to tell;
For the heart of the King is unsearchable.

Some glimpse at least of the end we glean,
Of the spiral curve and plan;
For, stretch as it may through the worlds unseen,
They are ever the worlds of man;

And—with all spaces—
Man's mind embraces
The way of the stairs as well:—
His heart, like the King's, is unsearchable.

OF THE DEEP SEAS

OF THE DEEP SEAS

ONE secret of the world is sadness,
  Granting tears at length are dried,
Set the cares that mar life's pages,
In the course of many ages,
  Once, and that for all, aside.

Take the heights and the abysses,
  Those great spaces which are past,
The great forward vistas, blending
With the dreams of life unending
  And immeasurably vast:

Surely joy, with all its keenness,
  Haunts too narrow grooves of change,
On the common sense of pleasure
Draws too much, to serve as measure
  Of the world's resource and range.

Morning stars may sing together,
  Sons of God for joy may shout;
But beyond the choric pæan
Spreads the stillness empyrean,
  Where the anthem falters out.

STRANGE HOUSES OF SLEEP

If we came and pass'd like summer,
   Short of sight though joy would be,
It might help us towards forgetting,
Twixt our rising and our setting,
   What a moth's-flight space have we.

But confronting earth's unearnest
   And yet ever anxious span
With the undeclared hereafter,
Joy must perish and light laughter
   Waver on the lips of man.

Life is so far past all searching,
   So much hangs from strings so frail,
That the firmest faith must question
And against all dark suggestion
   Hope can never quite prevail.

Love remains and Love may save us,
   Many keys of doom are there;
But if more with gladness blended
Than dejection deep attended,
   Those who love shall first declare.

Well then to be self-reliant,
   Highest ends with strength achieve,
Hold that life is best expounded
By the faith in goodwill grounded;
   So go forward, so believe.

But ask not that joy be with you ;
  Light things are by joy express'd :
Unto us the deeps are speaking,
Past the sadness of their seeking
  Is God's graveness and God's rest.

THE WIDER PROSPECTS

On level meads as smooth as garden lawns,
Rooks swarm with gleaming plumage, then with screams
Discordant rise and wheel awhile in air !—
God's splendour brightens now their peaceful flight,
To giant elms returning, dizzy nests
Poised in the air triumphant.

                                        Here my road
Reveals the open country. I see slopes
Of verdant green, wide fields and marshy lands
Low-lying ; I see misty hills against
The distant sky, in outline dimly limn'd—
A long blue line. The land is dark with trees,
Far and away beyond me winds the road,
Ascending ; as I follow, evermore
The prospect widens, round me hills and hills,

And round me all things in the clear, sweet air
Shine to the sunset light. The winds are held
By silver spells of silence.

The whole earth
Seems mine, and shortly will all heaven put forth
Stars o'er my path. Methinks this road so broad,
So brown, so pleasant, like the rover's life
Goes on for ever; it is steep, it curves,
It leaps, and dips; it follows all the vale,
Then takes a spiral course to climb the slope,
So to be lost amidst a world of downs.
Here silver willows in the evening wind
Begin to stir; by hedges do the oaks
Rich foliage rustle; on the open mead
A brown horse browses, while in one beyond
A stalwart beast with black and burnish'd sides
Slow drags a loaded wain to reach the track;
And at the bend he gains it. As I walk
Behind, a dry and subtle incense fills
The cool air round me; but I pass it now
And see the farm before me: so mine eyes
At every turn are met by something new
Which gratifies the senses and the mind.

All suddenly the golden air is changed
To purple, passing swiftly into grey,
And there is mist about me; it is chill;
The sense of sadness settles as I reach
A clear space free upon the West and pause

THE WIDER PROSPECTS

To mark the contrast of the dark green trees
Against a vivid and illumined sky,
Ere night one hour has fallen—O first star,
Whose lamp is kindled in the South so high !—
To mark it and to worship. Now the moon,
Out of the bleak mists of the East, aglow,
Without one touch of sadness, o'er the marsh
Her orb uplifts; how fair, how sweet, how blue,
Looks the high zenith, with faint clouds involved;
And as the summer breeze from flute-notes soft
Turns to a resonant wind and boldly calls
Among the echoing hills, my transient mood
Of graveness passes, for the night is strong,
And passionately the voices of the night
Speak to deep wells within the heart of man,
Till the deep wells make answer—I, at least,
Walking in summer on the winding road,
With downs about me, with the moon above—
With the bright moon which, as it rises, pours
A light increasing through the lilac sky—
Amidst the wine-like fragrance of the air,
Hear depth to depth make answer, height to height.

JOYS OF LIFE

THAT light we know to be only seeming;
Those stars in dream looking down on dreaming;
  Blank space which cheats us; quick time which
    slips;
Thin ghosts of wines which deride our yearning;
Pale shadows of love which leave us burning
  To gain the rapture of unseen lips:

The faiths too cold for the heart's subsistence;
Hope's light too faint on a bleak existence;
  All ways too many for ends in doubt:
But though perplex'd by disorder'd courses—
One strength call'd up from the soul's resources—
  Still to go on and to do without!

WATERS OF CREATION

THOU dost reflect alone the changeful skies—
A greater speculation fills our eyes:
  We are thy masters, we are more than thee;
Above thy wildest storm the mind can rise,
    Strong sea, great sea!

LOSS AND GAIN

LOSS AND GAIN

We lost it long ago; we dream not how,
We know not where. The spirit with a brow
From high thoughts radiant, and at peace in them,
Wore, as some say, its royal diadem;
But crowns are nothing to the soul and this
High legend only or a symbol is.
Ah, friends! What, therefore, did we lose and why?
Was it our home beyond the far blue sky?
But home is only where the soul, above
These anxious ways, finds sleep of perfect love,
While the same heaven which draws our hearts, we know,
Extends as far above us as below.
Whence, therefore, this so dimly understood
Yet haunting sense within us of the good
Wherein we once rejoiced; which evermore
Through mournful ways of life we now deplore?
Ah, if the heart could learn, the heart might find!
Or, at least, less inhibited and blind,
Move on more conscious where the ways direct,
What to avoid aware and what expect.
Here is the measure of our loss—perchance
One gain is ours who in the dark advance

STRANGE HOUSES OF SLEEP

As best we can, peering with hoodwink'd eyes—
Light comes at last more splendid, and surprise
The sweeter for the gloom and its dismay,
When night in fine and hoodwinks pass away:
A hand has guided and a hand shall lead
Till loss be loss no more, but gain indeed.

THE POWER AND THE GLORY

O WELL for those whose duty assumes the guise of beauty,
And well for those whose mission puts on the veils of grace;
For whom the wings they rise on are those Love also flies on,
Whom strongly God leads onward by light of fairest face:
To whom nine choirs of angels at dawn proclaim evangels
And words of peace at vesper time through channels such as Thou;
With glory on the lowly from holy place and holy
Of altar chaste, for shining placed—one radiant vestal brow!

FRAGMENTUM

FRAGMENTUM

I look behind on all my former life,
With its strange fortunes, feeling faint surprise,
Because with even mind, with chosen speech,
I muse thereon; while, sunk in deepest thought,
Thou standest by me, patient, unperturb'd.
Leaf-blinds are drawn, the late sun shines without
On wide green meadows; all this bower is fill'd
With things familiar. Thou, reserved and cold,
Dost hear my tale; how all things formal seem!
And yet what secret matters—O my friend,
What thoughts! What dark thoughts haunting
evermore!

A sudden flash, before the eyes of mind
Passing at times, takes all our heart away,
As rapture caught Elias; we are lost
To earth and time, far in some place of dream.
As sees the warden of the castle walls,
How stretch the pastures wide and darkling woods,
How the vales dimple, how the light streams wind,
What silver shining speaks of sea beyond—
So in light richer than our landscapes know,
Yon ocean splendour past all fair romance

Interprets its bright pictures to the heart
By words no more, but living images.
Once, from the realms thereof, we drew that light,
Exalting Nature; but the thoughts, my friend—
The dark, dread thoughts—the deeps behind the gleam,
And in those depths abysses, gloom unpierced!

Now that this avenue of trees is pass'd,
Take breath. The road slopes after; its descent
Is steep to reach the streamlet, and with stones
Made rough—to save the horses. Do you mark
That little bridge which spans the burn? Our path
Goes over it. Before us to the left
The old church looms; a growth of ivy there
Shows in the evening light its splendid green
On tower and nave. A dial all the day
Tells time in silence on the southern side.
Here swirls the shallow water; did you catch
That flashing fin? See, in this hole curl'd round,
A speckled eel is sleeping. So we reach
The long white-fronted house. Who dwells therein?
Patience! The water on a single side
Washes the ample lawn; at brink thereof,
Wide spreads the walnut tree, a stately growth,
Its broad, rich leaves above the waters drooping.
Peace, brother soul! here is the trysting-place.

Perchance things lesser in the end shall save
Things greater, and the least is also first.

VIATICUM

VIATICUM

He who hath made it will mend it,
He who began it must end it—
  Leave it to Him.
Weary and poor thou art,
Weak of purpose and frail in heart—
  Thy hopes are vague and dim.
Stretch forth thy hand and try
If thou canst touch the sky;
Lift up thine eyes and see
How far 'tis over thee—
  Exceeding reach!
Leave it—the hour is late—
Leave it to Him, to fate;
Great may take care of great,
  Each star of each!

Those books, my friend, you purchased yestereve,
  Though treating truthfully a certain art,
Contain not that you fondly now believe:—
  (Brother, a little while and we depart!)

That habitation by the mere and stream,
  For sylvan peace, self-promised long ago,
Will not afford the rest of which you dream:—
  (Come, lock up house, my friend, and leave it so!)

STRANGE HOUSES OF SLEEP

The wealth which took you hand in hand with sin—
When you stand knocking at a certain gate—
Will forge no golden key to let you in :—
(Make haste, one further step, the hour is late !)

Now, well-away ! What treasures some things were—
Ah, woe is mine !—which now are utter dross :—
(Toll slowly !—Stifle the unseemly stir—
A horror falls upon the house of loss !)

Be still, pale prophets of disaster, yet
In pace, in idipsum, dormiet !

OTHER MANHOODS

We know that ever from the birth thereof
Both earth and sea are sentiently alive
And in the cosmic harmony perform
A willing part, to holy law conform'd,
Sounding at times an individual note
Conceived within them through the starry hymn
Which—Ave, ave !—high creation chants.

OTHER MANHOODS

The leaf which shrivels in the hand must feel,
Though it be feebly, and the bud which lifts
Its head to catch the sunlight, we believe—
Since something in us prompts and forces faith—
Does know, though dimly, that the light and heat
Are life and health and happiness. Through all
That lives some form of consciousness pulsates
And not all blindly struggles towards the good,
Sharing some part of our humanity,
Seeking increase thereof. The joyous bird,
Which in the glare of this light-clouded sun
Pours forth his soul in music, is, we think,
In some way conscious of the power of song
And in a measurable way perceives
The beauty of it—in his own degree
Is therefore poet, since the gift is his,
The conscious use and simple love thereof.
In some translation of a later day,
Some evolution unto earth unknown,
Are any heights forbidden him?—Who knows?
This only—from the deeps within ourselves,
Above the common interests of sense,
Strange pasts at times well up, of leaf and bud,
And we who know not truly what we are
Know also not, yet guess, what once we were.

OF CONSUMMATION

Wise, O heart, is the heart which loves, but what
of the heart which restrains—
Not that it reckons the cost, preferring the ease to
the pains,
But knowing the great true gifts which are never
received or given,
An aching void being under love and over an
aching heaven.

Wise are the lips which have learn'd how long may
linger the lips' caress,
But wiser they who lingering lips can chasten and
repress,
For that which the fain mouth burns to kiss and
loving arms to embrace
Has never been given to lips or arms in the world
of time and space.

Wise therefore, and wise above all, is he who does
not swerve aside,
But knows to his greatest need on earth is service
of earth denied;

Who least things asking of flesh and blood and less
than the least of rest,
Goes on demanding the greater good and disdaining
the second best.

After much conquest and toil no doubt, but high
in his starry tracks,
Shall the greater ministers come to him burning the
sacred flax,
Saying, so passes the world and so the glory and
light expend,
But the High Term, follow'd unflinching, cries: I
can repay at the end.

IN ANY GARDEN

I

I DREAM'D in a garden when noon was past,
On a thyme-sweet bank reclining—
Half dream'd, half thought of the peace unbroken
After the breeze to the rose has spoken:
And ere it rises, where light so still is,
To breathe of love to the shining lilies.
Over the bower was the bindweed twining,

And beyond the lily's last white cup
Life's mystery yielded its secret up—
So the end seem'd clear at last—
As in any garden when noon is past.

II

They came who lead me, the sons of thought,
That ever my steps attend,
And the first is named the Sense of the End
But the second the Way that the End is sought:
Now as to the third, I have search'd my soul,
But I know not well, for his face is dim,
If love can divine the great name of him,
Yet I dream that his name is The Goal—
Say, have you also by these been taught?
Have you not seen them, from first to last,
In any garden, when noon is past?

THE KING'S SECRET

KEPT well—too closely kept—or so it seems—
Few quests disclose the secret of the King.
That presence, manifest in evening's cool
Long since in the first garden of the world,
Withdrawn to-day in the most secret place

THE INWARD MAJESTY

Of all concealment, baffles reason's search.
God veils his glory from our questing eyes :—
We know not why ; few claims are ours to press ;
But still the longing and the hope remain,
Poor baffled reason in the end perchance
Finds her spent forces unto new give place,
For in the soul at length, from all apart,
The glory dawns, and in the depths thereof
A still voice breathes the Secret of the King.

THE INWARD MAJESTY

OUR mental dalliance with the lighter vein
Is possible in cities of the plain,
  In pleasant meadows, or where gardens are ;
And on the fringe and margin of the sea,
Such happy refuge comes to you and me.
But compass'd by the immeasurable main,
Or on those heights where nothing intervenes
  Betwixt the climber and a certain star,
Let inward majesty to outward scenes
  So consciously respond,
That, when the shallows into silence fall,
The soundless deeps within the soul may call,
  And Words of Life make answer from beyond.

STRANGE HOUSES OF SLEEP

HAUNTINGS

From life's first dawn till now, when life's new
stress
Drives all things swifter into consciousness,
Earth has been full of those strange secret things
Which we touch sometimes in our quickenings.
So in the veils which commonly divide
From what we vaguely term the further side,
Rent or thin place makes possible to see
That which encompasses so pressingly.
There is no man, however steep'd in sense,
But can recall some such experience,
When dusk or dark or daylight dimly gave
Suggestions which are deeper than the grave,
Till soul in body for a moment felt
Contact with souls that in no flesh have dwelt.
'Tis then we know there is a houseless host
Of incomplete humanities, of ghost
And spectral people, who, from dregs and lees
And depths of stagnant and unconscious seas
Exhaled, their evolution's course begin,
But, though remote, are still our kith and kin,
And by the process of the years advanced
Shall reach, like us, their share of light enhanced.

HAUNTINGS

You cannot draw your blinds at eventide
And not shut thousands in the dark outside;
You cannot fling the windows wide at morn
But thousands enter, on the sunbeams borne:
Sad is their lot, midst all their crowds alone,
To none responding and by all unknown.
And yet the pity in the human heart
For life's great travail, of which theirs is part,
By solidarity of all things here,
Helps such poor souls, so far and yet so near;
Just as our kindness to the dear, dumb beasts
First hallows us, making us Nature's priests,
Then helps their prison'd yearning to assuage,
And lastly leads them in their pilgrimage.
Ah! pity, tenderness, and love—these three
And the Great God above—and these are He!

THE BRIDAL JOURNEY

He called her with a mighty cry:—
"Come forth! I need thee, eye to eye:
  Lo, all of mortal life I set
Aside for thee!" She, hearing, came—
A virgin soul of purest flame—
  And their eyes met.

STRANGE HOUSES OF SLEEP

From out her house of flesh came she;
He stood, a spirit grandly free
  From mortal veil and bond.
They left their bodies side by side—
The blessed bridegroom and the bride—
  And soar'd beyond.

The paths of light their presence own
And zones beyond the starry zone;
A light outshining suns for them
Was granted as a diadem,
And where no mortal steps have trod
They follow'd the high quest of God.

DREAMS OF DEATH

In storm, in darkness and in stress,
In languor and deep weariness,
What wonder if, o'er life's dark deep—
That tossing sea which dare not sleep—
From time to time on each should come
An exile's sickness for his home?

THE troubled sleep of man endures, it seems,
Long—and too long—laid waste with evil dreams
Which end not even with his latest breath,
And sad and lonely are the dreams of death.
May those who did with sleep of sense inbind
Vouchsafe, compassioning, to free the mind,

For heavy vapour doth the heart enring!
I, more than all, should pray for wakening—
These many years in mortal slumber kept.
What if, indeed, my time is overstept
And the great hour I should have known is past,
So that the only tenant in the vast
And silent place of sleep, in vain I beat
Wings weariful and weary hands and feet
Against the gates, with clamour and ado,
But there is no more hope of passing through!

If morn will come! It is so long to wait;
Long seem'd it never at the cottage gate—
That space of day the morn and night betwixt
When forth I went, and bore to lighten toil,
As hallows for the crowded day's turmoil,
My bride within the gate, an image fix'd,
Till eve and love should come to hearten me.

But I went forth one morning when the free
Spring breath found ambush in her sunny hair,
Which opulence of light encompass'd, there
Standing so statue tall, as saints might, crown'd,
And the child with her in the garden ground,
Where heavy scent of hyacinths abode
And dull'd the dusty tumult of the road:
An artless picture, yet of equal grace
With any sacrament of angel's face;
And in my soul, as in the street, it stirr'd
The solemn music of that secret word

Which Nature must not utter lest she cease.
So as I pass'd abroad, with inward peace,
All suddenly methought that it was long
Betwixt the Matins time and Evensong;
Then, midst a strange confusion in the mind
At many cries before me and behind,
I knew that I should go back never more—
That never gate should open as before,
Nor door swing back, nor scented dusk reveal
The eyes which welcome and the hands which heal—
Being by sad calamity or sin
Absorb'd for ever by the gulf within;
And, disinherited of earthly shape,
Doom'd self in self to find, nor e'er escape
Even by plunging deeper in the gloom—
Such is the unlighted secret of my tomb.

Long have I sought, yet no relief is found,
And my soul sickens in this aching round,
Amidst the purblind air and vapours dim;
But it is idle now to call on Him
Who having put to sleep, as I have said,
Is our sole hope of waking from the dead
And all the ghostly semblances which fill
With their own dread the halls of voided will.

O then I pray that I may find some track
At least to my old life directing back,
And that my dreaming arms may there enfold
The wife who shared with me the sleep of old,

DREAMS OF DEATH

The little child whose innocence and mirth
Seem'd newly waken'd in the life of earth
Rather than aught which play'd in dreams of
sleep.

There is an anthem full of meaning deep
Which evil thought from souls entranced could
drive,
And save from phantoms of the night alive;
There is a promise which from old has said
How rest from labour on the blessed dead
In peace descends: Give me their balm once
more,
And they, perchance, repeated o'er and o'er,
Shall yet become to me a gospel word,
With grace to die hereafter in the Lord.

Ah, let us rest as much as men may do
Those faithful homes within where hearts are true,
Because—without—the darkness and the cold
Hide laidly shapes and monstrous growths from view,
And hard it fares with those who shall behold!

STRANGE HOUSES OF SLEEP

WORLDS OF DREAM

THE sun descended in a flaming mist
And all the world beneath it—wide, waste downs,
Blue sky—serene and beautiful—and thou,
Half-shrouded sea, mysterious, with smooth,
Far-reaching bay, for miles and miles the land
Embracing—steep'd therein, divinely glow'd
Through deepening orange clouds . . . A sudden
change,
A shifting wind, a lifting mist—and lo!
Eastwards the sea shone cold and steely grey,
While downs and headlands, with the chalky roads
That wound among them, as the wan, white moon
Rose over like a phantom grandiose—
All these grew sombre. Facing there the main,
I stood, the Sunset Land upon my right,
With capes and cliffs, with towns and towers therein,
Enchanted dreaming; on the left, this world,
Which sober'd sadly towards a single tint
As night fell down thereon. It did not sleep,
It did not wake, but ever as the wind
Grew keener, utter'd its disquietude,
Sole sign of life. Of which of these could one
Apart from both, in such a mood, have said
This and not that was true reality?

IN THE ELEGIAC MANNER

IN THE ELEGIAC MANNER

Now Autumn crisps and dries the yellow'd leaf,
  Long since sad reapers brought the harvest in;
All which dejects us or exalts is brief—
  Death in life's mask, shall life in death's begin?

Say, one is gone—perchance a kindly face,
  A voice perchance which could some hearts encheer—
Haunt not, vain elegy, his former place
  And, vacant heart, forbid the falling tear!

Trite epitaphs—"Too good on earth to bide"—
  Let fools inscribe. Did peace make sweet his end?
Who knows?—*Implora pace!* Turn aside
  From hackney'd thoughts of father and of friend.

Convention tolls its bell with mournful sound,
  Convention plumes the hearse which bears the clay,
Convention cries that hearts in hallow'd ground
  Embalm remembrances that ne'er decay.

Go to! the heart forgets, the heart shall die,
  Go to, who cares that dust to dust returns?
Or that in chapels of mortality
  Some little space the lamp of memory burns!

STRANGE HOUSES OF SLEEP

Leave these old follies! Down the silent halls
  And the long avenues that soul has pass'd,
If you have strength, refrain from useless calls
  To other meetings—what if this were last?

That matters nothing, so he reach his goal:
  Call, therefore, in the great Augustan mood
Once and for all such end to crown his soul,
  Content, so he bear that, to bear your rood.

A HARD SAYING

UNSELFISH love which would itself fulfil
Must be what men call mean, must make unask'd
The first advances, and a cold response,
Rebuffs and misconceptions overlook,
To prosecute its end, which is to give,
For love's best reasons, unrequited, all
Love's heart and life's devotion.

                                        This confess'd,
Some brief indulgence let the heart enjoy—
From thought set free, from all the weary weight
Of those great ends whereto, since early days
Elected, souls must strive and, striving, see
New fields of labour opening far beyond

Into the infinite. Then, Love, awhile,
From heights descending, unto some green place,
Like this, in vernal hours or in the soft
Luxuriant summer prime, from high degrees,
Exemption find—and take the grade of peace,
Renouncing not; with all our doom foreseen,
Such respite gives the greater strength to bear,
Puts by the sense of whole unworthiness,
Or lifts it up into our aid unask'd
Who cannot choose but deem our souls unmeet,
O Love of all! for love of thine and thee,
Yet only love us, and in love like thine,
Our soul's love-flaming shall be meet to hold—
O love beyond all love! the love of thee.

THE SWOONING CASTLE

SUDDENLY wide in the night awake—
Do you know what that means?—with a start
  And a tremulous heart,
  In the dark of the night woke I:
Had a voice unknown of a day to break
  Utter'd some warning cry?
But the East was cold and the thin white fold
Of a light mist up to the windows roll'd

And the leaves by the windows wept.
'Tis a mournful thing, at a time so dead,
To wake uncall'd and with stealthy tread
And the hush'd breath backward kept,
From room to room, in the curtain'd gloom,
Pass, and from bed to bed.

They slept:
Some in their peace and some in their grace,
And some there were with a haunted face
And a fever'd head.
Once at the corridor's end I drew
To a sheeted figure which glided through
To the top of a stairway steep:
It carried a darken'd lamp and pass'd:
There was none in the house that slept so fast
As he who walk'd in his sleep.
Over the stairs I peer'd and found,
With head to breast, by his lantern's side,
On the porter's bench was the porter bound,
I knew not whether in sleep or swound,
And heavy-eyed by the doorway wide
Lay drowsy henchman and dreaming hound.
With none to challenge, I slipp'd the latch
And, passing under the streaming thatch,
I visited stable and stall and stye,
But I never came on an open eye,
For the roosting fowl that crow'd unbidden
Slept with his beak in his plumage hidden.

THE SWOONING CASTLE

Far and sad in a world of reeds
A shoal brook slipp'd through the marsh and meads,
With no more sound than the dark lagoon,
Dead still, outstaring the dripping moon;
The moon on her side in the mist lay red—
Green leaves, but they stirr'd not overhead!
So, seeing the swoon of the world outside
  Has more of sorrow and less of kin
Than the torpid heart of the house within—
Like the hush which falls when a ghost has cried—
My heart with its yearning drew me back,
By the creaking stairway's winding track.
In an upper room of the roof which faces
  East, with the sense of a hope subdued
That a light may whiten the mist-fill'd spaces,
  Sleep being out of my thoughts, I brood
And watch, but I feel that they watch me too—
The unseen ones, sitting the long night through—
Near, as it may be, though out of reach,
Till the sleepers waken to life and speech
  At the end of this sorrowful spell.
And seeing that high in the belfry tower
  There hangs a listless bell,
Some voice may bid me proclaim the hour:
Whence in my comfortless mood I gain
The sense of a vigil not wholly vain.
Shall I not, seeing the Rising Sun,
Cry: "Look: It is Morning"—when night is done?
If I fell at the end into slumber deep,
I should call out such good news in my sleep.

STRANGE HOUSES OF SLEEP

HOW IT FALLS BY THE SEA

THE air was cool, the wind was fresh, the sky
Before him violet, westward tinged with deep
And angry red. Behind him, loose and black,
Great clouds roll'd up; the church impending loom'd;
He pass'd with awe beneath its tower of stone—
Square, tall and grey—the graveyard cross'd in haste
And reach'd the wood; beyond its gentle slope
Far stretch'd a plain; and there the early mists
Had gather'd; from the orange of the West
A dull glow fell on quiet pool and pond;
The lamps in scatter'd hamlets there and here
Began to glisten. All his later way
The scarlet sunset and the stormy South
Made splendid, and with images sublime
The boy's mind fill'd; while o'er his head the pale
Translucent vault of heaven was thinly sown
With gleaming stars; while o'er the sea the pure
Unclouded moon her white and perfect disc
Reveal'd, suffusing light sky-wandering clouds
And ether's pensive lilac.

HOW IT FALLS BY THE SEA

By the shore
He paused, the waters washing at his feet,
But in the distance, mingling with the wind,
Giving forth solemn sounds. And turning then,
One mile or more, against the breeze he kept
His set face steadfast. By his path the pale
And modest silverweed, midst stones, maintain'd
A struggling life. A mile or more, the waves
Charm'd him with music, and the moon still wax'd
Above the trembling bosom of the deep.
A mile or more, he watch'd that sphere dilate
Till thin clouds veil'd it, till it show'd alone
A pallid phantom. Then the sun burst forth
Amidst the bank of black foreboding cloud,
Drooping long tendrils down of angry light;
He stood, the blaze upon his cheek and brow
Smote him. One moment every field and tree—
The haystacks and the hedges and the thatch
Of cottages—shone in that gorgeous light
As things transfigured. Suddenly the sun
From out the ruins of the purple cloud
Fell swift; the twilight over distant hills
And low champaign in utter gloom devolved.

Awhile the waning glory of the West—
The broken pageant and the shards thereof—
He watch'd; the sullen purple, tinged with gold,
Grew lurid; leaden vapours far away
Were stain'd with blood; but here and there the sky
Laid bare far depths of melancholy blue.

STRANGE HOUSES OF SLEEP

The boy turn'd northward, down a lane which led
Straight from the sea. Beside some stunted elms
He paused; the darkness chill'd him; far and near
He heard the chafing of the incessant waves,
As suddenly a night of gloom involved
Their vast expanse, and he, more lone than they,
Knew well how night discourses to the soul.
He started, as a bird, with whirring wings,
Broke forth from covert. The wind died and rose,
But darkness deepening on the early wheat,
Left every green blade visible: his path
Wound pale before him; waver'd stars above;
And still the phantom of the moon behind
Mourn'd at him as he pass'd into the night.

TO OTHER ENDS

Look forth no more where bindweeds creep
    About thy lattice bars,
And move no more where waters sweep
    Entranced by musing stars!
Thy peace be full, thy rest be deep,
    Dark night possess thine eyes;
While night as dark is ours who weep,
    Sweet Life, fill other skies:
That which God join'd to make thy wonder,
For Heaven's gain, thus He puts asunder.

BURDENS OF BABYLON

BURDENS OF BABYLON

WHEN the stars cease to speak to thee ; when all
The silent messages which softly fall
From liquid skies, over dark groves, have said
Their final word ; when ministries are dead,
When winds are voiceless and, from distance brought,
Sea sounds give up no more the form of thought ;
Then faded Nature, once in life so glad,
Wears sadder mien than ever mourner had ;
And if one utterance in the world is yet,
'Tis but the burden of a vain regret.

When with a melancholy, helpless trend,
All settles slowly into silent end,
Then the soul also, fickle and deranged,
Too weak for action and from peace estranged,
If offer'd straightway an immortal cup
Would lack the power of hand to lift it up ;
Then hearts no longer struggle to get breath,
But through deep lethargy subside towards death ;
And underneath the swooning moon or sun
There comes no help for any, no not one ;

STRANGE HOUSES OF SLEEP

While of all things that are of least avail,
Love, which we lean'd on, is the first to fail.
Yet, signs and sacraments of death, bereft
Of death's bleak graces, is there nothing left?

O inexpressible! O deeps forlorn!
O wild clouds, collocated eve and morn!
O eyes, imparting through their glooms a sense
Of vast abysses of impenitence,
With gulfs behind of sorrow unreveal'd
And bitter springs of loss in gulfs unseal'd!
Say, is there nothing? Do ye hold at length
Far off suggestions of some fount of strength—
Far as the stars of peace o'er stars of strife,
And far as life is from the life of life?

Wrecks on the tide-ways, wrecks upon the sea;
Black frozen heights wherein no breath can be;
Hearts that have broken, hearts in ardent heat
To ashes burnt—vain ways and vain conceit—
Yes, through immeasurable loss and need,
Come hints of One still strong to intercede,
And to the prostrate soul in poison'd lands
Comes grip of the unseen, uplifting hands.

ONWARD

BEYOND the breakers lies the free,
Unfathomable space of sea;
Beyond the sea the harbour far;
And that beyond new countries are.
From cliff to hill, from hill to plain,
We pass and find a further main;
Until we reach where time is not,
Brothers! But then beyond it—what?
Peace, doubting heart which questions thus—
Peace! Do not all things answer us?
Or if they speak not, all and each,
Silence gives deeper hints than speech.

GABRIEL

Do you remember, wheresoe'er you keep
Your contact with eternity, asleep
Or waking, but at least transported now
Beyond such light as stars to earth allow,

And so, I trust, set free from time and space—
Do you remember his unearthly face
Shining so softly in the temple's band?
If I spoke riddles, you would understand
Who are—I pray!—intelligence unmix'd;
But even then the deeper sense you fix'd
And saw with me great miracles in him,
White-vested walking through the cloisters dim.
Then, knowing that none except yourself above,
With me below, will penetrate our love,
However plainly stands the written word,
Let me conceal no more, whose heart is stirr'd
To tell outright what then I spoke alone
Either to you, apart in undertone,
Or but in parables to other men.
Far have we travell'd both 'twixt now and then;
You, as I dream, are something more than earth,
Brought through cold deeps of death to your new birth,
While I have follow'd for so long the shades
And lights reserved in strange and secret grades
For few indeed, that, set from man apart—
In spite of all corruptions of the heart—
Pursuing a peculiar path of quest,
Shunn'd am I or forgotten by the rest.

As in your ear then, plainly let me tell
When first it was we look'd on Gabriel,
At mass or vespers, guarded, earnest, blythe,
A white-robed, censer-bearing acolythe;

GABRIEL

Only a face amidst an incense cloud—
Silent within the chants which swell'd so loud.
Lovely he was, as human beauty goes—
The lily's lustre, the faint blush of rose,
Met in his face; his lips were chaste as fair
And a dim nimbus was his auburn hair,
While his deep eyes had caught, as in a net,
All the dark glories of the violet.
Youth though he was, in our two hands we could
Have ta'en his face to kiss as lovers should,
But on his earthly presence had come down
So high a sense of vision and of crown,
That out of any place where lovers lean
And whisper, he, with his uplifted mien,
So bright uprose that, like the ground he trod,
We knew him seal'd and set apart to God.

As Dante standing in the market-ways,
Who saw his blest Madonna many days,
But did, continually spell'd, defer
Each opportunity of speech with her;
We with the boy adored the sacred host
But challenged not that spiritual ghost—
Until at length his apparition ceased.
This day, perchance, a consecrated priest,
He celebrates, all fairly alb'd and stoled,
The holy mass at which he served of old.
Well, you are dead, and God is strong to save,
But certain secret matters to my grave

STRANGE HOUSES OF SLEEP

I carry heavily concerning you,
Who were through all so good and more than true;
Still in your heart make them a safe retreat,
If you can do so, at the judgment-seat.
But through the sorrows of your later years,
That boy's face hallow'd you for purer spheres;
'Mid derelictions of my longer road,
So has it also with myself abode;
Still in the vigils of a wakeful night
It serves like prayer because it shines so white,
And brings in ushering to slumber deep
Some of their peace who fall in Christ asleep.

Old friend, whate'er our early verse may tell,
Here is the mystery of Gabriel;
But the rare seeds sown thus in earth of ours
Once gave us many miracles of flowers;
Fair fruits too promised—what of these to say?—
Oh, you are dead, and he has gone away!

MIRRORS OF MANHOOD

Man's soul itself beholds in every glass
   And its own speech discerns in every tone;
All Nature voices what he is and was
   And will be—equally in star or stone.

MIRRORS OF MANHOOD

Man gives its parable to every stream ;
If "running brooks" are books, he writes, he reads ;
If stones are sermons, he provides their theme,
And with himself in these he speaks, he pleads.

No living tongue but his was ever heard ;
Still Nature stood till he, an exile, came,
Bringing dim echoes of an older word
And fragments of a now unutter'd Name.

For though he speaks and speech imparts to all,
That which he would he cannot tell nor learn,
And pale reflections of his own long call
Tortures, their inward meaning to discern.

His outward tumult fills his ears in vain
And down his own vast depths in vain he cries :
Perchance the still profoundities explain
That which exceeds all words, however wise.

Perchance his speech withdrawn from things outside
And all resounding caverns hushed within,
That which the clamours from his soul divide
May to draw nigh and to commune begin.

STRANGE HOUSES OF SLEEP

SEVEN WATCHERS

A CERTAIN Son of the Desire which springs
From life's heart-deeps unfathom'd towards the things
Withdrawn in undetermined altitude,
Sat in his silence shrouded and subdued,
On many fragments of his splendid dreams—
Vocations shadow'd forth by ardent schemes—
And haunting insights—pondering alone.
But the height's secrets are a world unknown,
And though we recognise in these our rest,
That which we look to find—has heart express'd
Save in the glowing symbols of the heart?
Therefore the quest seems vague, and far apart
Desire stands, vainly reaching towards its end:
So deeper glooms than with the night descend
Fell on the soul of that aspiring Son.

Thereat, a little space, and after, One
Who entered softly in the gloom and fill'd
A seat beside him, said: "Perchance He will'd
To keep us doubtful of the soul's true aim;
But there are earthly gifts—and these are Fame
And Wealth and Honour and all high estate."
"I also enter'd by that barren gate,"

The Son of Heaven replied, "and surely found
By what strange sorrows is ambition crown'd."
"Yea," said the other, "and I wait as well."

To these a third came in, made visible
By shining eyes—and spake: "The ways of Love
Are to be counted, as I deem, above
All earthly paths, and he who enters them
Has life in fulness and the diadem."
The Son made answer: "Hast thou counted Loss?"
And he: "My sorrow is my crown and cross;
The tears of Loss are bitter as the sea,
And, sword in heart, I also wait with thee."

Then silence follow'd till a fourth broke in,
Flush'd from the revel, singing: "I am Sin,
And I have known all raptures and the bliss
Of shame which meets with shame, to mix and kiss."
Then said the Son of the Desire which lifts
The heart in search of the unearthly gifts:
"What wages, brother, doth thy rapture earn?"
"From death they come and unto death return,"
The child of Bacchus and the Mœnads cried,
"And many deaths in life my soul has died;
But I will wait with thee for evermore."

"Kings of the earth," said One, who through the
door
Had enter'd suddenly, "and crowns of such,
May haply melt to ashes at a touch,

But Knowledge treasures still its proud estate,
And Wisdom's shining grows from less to great."
"O fair, sweet friend! What therefore knowest
thou?"
Spake the First Watcher. But with bended brow
The other answer'd—yea, with eyes which burn'd:
"That dust for ever has to dust return'd;
I also therefore wait dejectedly,
And Truth, though out of sight, perchance is nigh."

There follow'd him who said: "Though all things
fail,
Faith's sacred consolations still avail."
"Yea," said the Son, "did we indeed believe,
The star and dust perchance should interweave;
But the star also into dust may fall."

A deeper silence fill'd that gloomy hall,
And gloom was on the watchers, while the feet
Of hurried passers died along the street.
So all that night the solemn guard was kept:
Some pray'd within them sobbingly, some wept,
As they that melt towards prayer, and other some
Through windows look'd to see if morn would
come.
But the air gave up at the darkest hour
A sudden sense of presence and of power,
And where the six had waited through the night,
There stood a Seventh with a guiding light;

LOOKING WESTWARD

Who said: May peace be with you! I have been
Through the great gates of death, and I have seen
That which I testify as surely true.
Give me your hands, for I am made as you,
And look into mine eyes, and speak my Name."
Whereat the Watchers cried with one acclaim:
"Master of All, for Thee we waited long
Who to enlighten and to save art strong."
He answer'd: "Watch with me a little space!"
But they stood raptured, gazing on his face,
So that the world and all therein went by,
And from the eastern heaven the sun rose high.

LOOKING WESTWARD

WORLDS beyond worlds of sunset pageantry—
Wild West: the spirit with a yearning deep
Springs forth to thee! Like ripples are thy long
Low lines of violet cloud: all dreams, all hopes
Seem possible within these earthly bounds
Which heaven enrings and thy bright belt of light
Set in cerulean circle, jewel-wise.

THE END WHICH CROWNS

The music falters on the harp of gold;
That which it longs to say is never told,
Stern silence has received it evermore.
The thought which scarcely to the heart before
Was half so keenly or so highly given,
Once and for all to speak the heart has striven;
Once and for all the heart has failed therein.
The word and music of the word begin,
But cannot finish; yet the soul shall see;
Light in the soul has dawn'd, that light shall be
Extended surely through its great domain,
Nor towards the summits turn her eyes in vain—
Far end, perchance, but she can see the end.
Clouds intervene indeed and veils extend,
But gifted inly by those ardent rays,
Clouds and the veils thereof before the gaze
Of soul dissolving, shall the soul descry
That which is hidden from the fleshly eye,
The end and high significance of things.
Of old, great Plato said the soul has wings,
And deem not thou that ne'er the soul has risen,
Flame-wing'd, above the portals of her prison;

THE END WHICH CROWNS

Think not with bolts and bars she strives in vain,
Who can at need the path of stars attain;
Yet it remains that, stars and heights explored,
Or wheresoe'er the soul has plunged and soar'd,
In deep abysses or on holy hill,
One secret baffles and eludes her still.

Made subject now to terms of time and space,
Drawn by the outward, not the inward place,
She chiefly shares the public pomps and shows:
There star as shining star no secret knows,
Nor sun divines it. Earth has mighty themes
To guard our sleeping and our waking dreams,
The height has ravishment, the great sea-deep
Has lesser mysteries, to yield or keep;
That which we lack, the meaning and the goal,
Exceeds their depth and height. And hence the soul,
By outward witcheries encompass'd, sees
The glory and the glamour which are these:
She listens, she divines as best she can,
And gathers something of the cosmic plan,
While from the snatches of the secret caught,
Beyond the limit of the world of thought
Withdrawn in regions of which none can tell,
She fashions answers in an oracle
And burning prophecies which inly stir—
She fashions answers, nothing answers her.

Therefore of how it shall at length befall,
The hidden meaning and the end of all—

STRANGE HOUSES OF SLEEP

The secret—these are hidden from the soul,
Which gleans in part but cannot grasp the whole.
Some voices truly at her door have sung,
But in an unintelligible tongue;
And flashes sometimes from her centre strike
Which seem to show her what the end is like,
But all at best is vague and undeclared.
One lesson haply might her toil have spared:—
That which can answer nothing, or, if heard,
Only some unintelligible word,
Serving for presage in divining art,
May after all have little to impart;
But in the soul itself, if deeply sought,
Will come an answer to her inmost thought.

Let therefore music fail from harps of gold;
Let words be kept within the heart untold;
And let the soul no longer use her wings
For ranging through the outward scheme of things,
But inward turn the light of shining eyes—
Perchance the end is there, the meaning wise.

THE PALACE OF LIFE

THE PALACE OF LIFE

MAN's sacramental house has many halls
And secret passages contrived in walls,
With darken'd chambers, suited for repose,
In quiet corridors remote from those
Wherein the guests and menials daily tread.
Sad rooms are set for watchers by the dead,
And secret alcoves plann'd on lonely stairs
Open, wherein fond lovers unawares
Are seldom taken by the stealthy spy.
There also towers and turrets are built high,
Where those ascend whom solitary thought
Has inward contemplation's sweetness taught.
Halls of convention may be found and vast
Saloons for banqueting and music; last,
There, too, are chapels of a thousand creeds,
By hearts devoted to the greater needs,
And solemn places more remote than these
Wherein adepts set forth their mysteries.

Now, howsoe'er a man his life divide
'Midst things of sanctity or things decried,
One corner cover'd by the dome alone
Can knowledge or mere rumour make his own;

Yet in that house are casements opening
On vistas of the strange and unknown thing
Which spreads without humanity's abode.
Where lead the paths therein? Where leads the road?
What lies beyond the fastness and the fell,
Or the great deeps of sea which surge and swell?
O mists of valleys and æonian snows!
O desperate days and nights without repose!
There is no man that knoweth, save a dream
Shall hint him somewhat of the direful scheme;
Or voices equally unknown outseek
The watcher on his balcony, and speak
A message in his shrinking ear, about
The joy or sorrow that is stored without.
Whereafter visions and the power of song,
With deep prophetic tongues, to him belong;
Or, by desirable and awful things
O'erwhelm'd, his body from the house he flings,
When in a twinkling of the eye he learns
The all or nothing, but at least returns
Into the mansion of mankind no more.
The house has seemingly no public door
For coming and for going; here the dead
Sleep in the vaults beneath with easy head;
Or if their souls into the unpierced space
Go forth, the watcher cannot see their face;
And if at times against the windows press
Poor phantom aspects full of dreariness,
The horror of the eyes for those within
Cuts off the sympathy of kith and kin.

THE PALACE OF LIFE

Now this is, therefore, to dissuade a few
From heeding tidings, whether false or true,
Which in these later days are rumour'd round—
To say some open portal has been found,
Or one which can be open'd by the hand,
And entrance made into the unknown land;
That Nature high exalted then is seen;
That dead men greet us with a front serene;
That when the secret mazes have been trod
A man may find himself alone with God,
And can see truth and beauty with his eyes.
In sooth we know not which way beauty lies,
Or on what heights and in what wells and deeps
Truth, which is also beauty, wakes or sleeps,
Much less of how it shall the soul befall
In this place or in that to find the All.
But not denying that a door may be
Set back by him who hath its master-key,
Let one who, ere the ending of his days,
Has much endured and travail'd in strange ways,
Exhort his brothers not in life's short span
To leave unqualified the roof of man,
Or seek, especially in ways unknown,
What it may feel like when with God alone.
Our sacramental house has veils undrawn
And curtains never raised at eve or dawn;
It burns alone the instituted lights
And all that shows therein are only rites.
We know indeed the soul with her strong fires
Beyond these human ministries aspires

In spirit and in truth to reach her end;
But not in vain do veils the soul defend;
Nor yet in vain do nature, grace and art,
Their ceremonial formulæ impart;
And not in vain does God his glory dim
By many clouds that we can gaze on Him.
A time may come when He shall put them by,
And standing lip to lip and eye to eye,
From all conventions sign the soul's release,
With true *Pax tecum* and with kiss of peace
More closely married than is rhyme with rhyme.
Great is the speech of parables meantime,
And up and down the house of man there pass
The sacred pageants of a life-long mass:
O let the arid speculations end
Till from the altar steps the priests descend.

There is indeed a certain narrow road
Which in a sense leads forth from our abode,
But not by ways from vantage points descried
Through desert places of the world outside.
Open it lies for those to walk therein
Who having put away the life of sin,
With the long quest of their desire and gain,
Do in their own souls seek and so attain
The individual knowledge of their end.
Peace on those paths for the elect attend!
May the great universe expand for them
Through many kingdoms to their diadem!

And underneath the white light of their crown
May those who go to God find God come down,
Since in the secret centre of their heart
Who came from Him from Him did never part.
But howsoe'er encompass'd by the hosts
This is the life of life and not of ghosts,
Nor does it lie beyond the walls of each.
Hard is this path to learn of, hard to reach
And few there are that seek it, or can teach
The rending of the veils that guard it here,
Too well protected since it lies too near.
Therein the waking comes, the rest is dream;
Yet this is also in the mystic scheme
And steep'd awhile in life's magnetic trance
The souls that slumber may in sleep advance
And something still behold through their smoked lens—
Sic salve, Domine omnipotens!

THE SECRET GARDEN

Friends, it is fair in garden bowers conceal'd,
When round the high, fruit-heavy mural shield
  The white wind washes and the corn-fields roll;
But further still in the wide world afield,
  I found a secret garden of the soul.

STRANGE HOUSES OF SLEEP

O, there is morning glory on the sea,
And fragrant still at eve shall pinewoods be!
  While night is grand on mountains, in the glow
And mystery of moonlight; but for me
  One place reserve, of all the world I know!

So having travell'd long, and fain to rest,
I keep that place a secret in my breast
  And secret more than all one bower of love,
Where sweeter far than Araby the blest
  My spikenard giveth forth the fumes thereof.

BACK TO THE LAND

To silent worlds of music, open'd up
By audible solemnities of sound,
My soul escaped, and traversed endless groves
Of immemorial melody. A storm
Of choral praise, unprefaced, with a crash
Burst on me then, the language of dead gods,
And drew me back among the Temple's types—
Sign-words and sacraments of mystery.
So to the end it held me, magnet-wise,
Till thyrsis-bearers pass'd and hierophants;
But when the vacant Temple held alone
The secret god, I follow'd from afar
Behind the veil into the vestibule,

BACK TO THE LAND

And saw the ashes of the charcoal fire
Shew one faint spark; the open window shew'd,
All bent and twisted through the floral wilds,
A woodland path whence myrrh-like odours came;
Low voices came from violets and faint
Song-bursts of birds invisible.
By such
High offices, the heart, whose seeing sense
Follows election, having Nature heard
As Nature speaks, has taken to itself
A certain message and the most withdrawn—
To wit, those words within the common scope
Of speech. Thereafter, in pursuit of signs
More eloquent, of higher speaking things,
The heart takes counsel with the sanctuary
And finds the Holy of the Holies, past
All Holy Places, yet at times looks forth,
When all the chancels of the world without—
Which after their own manner sang of old—
Do now in likeness of his voice intone.
The chancel walls, expanding thereupon,
Take Nature in; exalting Nature gives
At every point upon the Temple's gates;
And if the fires and lights expend therein,
Her lights, her fires, assume on his behalf
The offices, not antiphons alone
Reciting, but responses order'd well.
If therefore priests at altars fall asleep.
And in their stalls the choirs forget the Rites,
No psaltery is wanting in the world.

STRANGE HOUSES OF SLEEP

A RITE OF EXALTATION

I THOUGHT at length that haply human love
Might offer refuge from the things above
Which had so long pursued my life ill-starr'd
Up pathways inaccessible—or hard,
At least to climb; and having climb'd, 'tis still
More dreadful on the summit of such hill
The mind's fastidious balance to preserve,
Nor dizzily towards precipices swerve
And the emerited soul in sense immerge.
Back therefore from the summit and the verge,
Where terribly the known and unknown meet,
For some few seasons baffled, such retreat
As those can make who once the starry track
Have strain'd at and for ever must look back,
I made, my peace with Nature, long foregone,
Sign'd, as I best could sign, and so put on
Once more the huddled vesture of my kind.
Then the unearthly beauties, which to find
I strove so long, for me seem'd now to strive;
Their tincture haunted all things here alive,
Suggesting ends desired that were not they;
And that which in the height was far away
On earthly eyes seem'd momently to loom—
Clamour of triumph seized, glorious doom.

A RITE OF EXALTATION

Then in the place of stillness, brooding deep
On frozen summits, and the awful sleep
Which can the soul amidst the heights enfold,
All that which beats within the chains of gold
And iris prison of the public things,
Through mystic music, its invisible wings,
Amidst the outward melodies, began
To speak as Nature never spoke to man.

I testify that past mere sense alone
Experience spreads her more exalted zone;
That past the common range of human mind
There stretch the royal regions undivined,
An undiscovered country which if trod
Seems to lead backward and be lost in God.
There is a door, which could we find its key,
Opens therein from our humanity.
So forth on roof and parapet at times
Stealing, I saw what none can speak in rhymes;
But never came the message to mine ear,
Or saw the visionary eye so near
As when, reluctantly, its potent spell
Breaking, I turn'd from the invisible
And brought the light of all that dwells withdrawn,
The glory of the spiritual dawn,
These fleshly regions to illuminate.

Now, there was one who dwelt within the gate
Of outward dreams, nor ever question'd these,
But rather, awestruck, from realities

Had surely shrunk, if face to face with them.
Yet beauty wore she as a diadem,
And shone in innocence a radiant star:
Gentle and mild was she, as maidens are
Whose souls are subtly link'd with things above
By sanctified capacities of love.
Her from the sons and daughters of the race
I chose, to lift up from her lonely place
Amidst the crowd which sees not where it goes:—
I wrought love's work on her, and now she knows.

What follows?—This—that soul can soul uplift;
Those who have dwelt in light can bring that gift
To something more than isolated fruit
Within themselves, and can at will transmute
Such as they take into their heart of heart,
Making an altar set from earth apart,
Whereon is kindled an eternal flame,
And there the Incommunicable Name
Is utter'd. Or—all symbols set aside—
Learn, simple woman can be deified!
I show this truth—when one, of light possess'd,
Has all his nature to the task address'd;
Know too the work is love's—and love's the call—
While love is also the material.
And at the end such union comes at length
As to the worker brings another strength
Those heights forsaken once again to dare,
Those realms discover which await him there,
With consciousness of ends beyond them still—
The holy palace, the eternal hill!

PLAY SCENES

NATURE is pantomime; some force bestirs
The antic struggles of her characters,
And semblances of life imparts to each,
But no true motion and no gift of speech:
Some mask unknown stands at the stage's wings
And for each mimic actor speaks or sings,
While in the galleries and stalls we sit
But do not rightly catch one word of it.

ABSOLUTION

HERE to me friends!—Have I wrong'd you?—Come
to me more than all—
That which my lips would utter, with tenderer lips
forestall,
Now that the wardens who watch'd me, breaking the
guard they kept—
(Passion and pride)—permit me—(dry-eyed among
those that have wept
No longer)—to weep as ye once wept—set free in a
sense—
Human amidst the human, not as a rock of offence:

The wand has smitten the rock and a plenteous water
springs,
So that my heart is link'd with the pulse at the heart
of things.

Ye that are human, pardon! If any I need forgive,
Rest I wish them and joy, with the life that a man
would live
Who, in spite of adverse omens written on earth and
sky,
Knows well that his Saviour liveth and redemption
draweth nigh.

Ye that in secret below your coats and plumage and
skins,
Shelter hearts which are human, free from our follies
and sins;
Birds of the air and the beasts, I know by your moans
and cries,
Your songs which pant for language, your sad, deep,
eloquent eyes;
Ye also have needed love, the want of the world ye
know;
Warm be the sunshine about you, soft the winds as
they blow;
If I have wrong'd you—it may be—come ye also—
forgive;
The life of all life uplift you, that ye may also live!

ABSOLUTION

Nature, gracious of seeming, we have met perchance
too late,
Truly to love each other, closely to mingle and mate;
But, in these latter days, less now than we were out
of reach,
In part I divine your thought, and in part you have
learn'd my speech;
So far as my life has wrong'd you—I pray you also,
forgive—
Some one has wounded you surely; may you be heal'd
and live!

Grace, from a world pour'd down which I knew in
the times of old,
Or ever my star was barter'd, or ever my birthright
sold;
Surely I loved thee always, wherever my steps have
stray'd;
To leave is still to love thee; I loved thee, though I
betray'd!
For all my wrongs forgive me, and here, in this
empty heart,
Till it fills, pour down thine unction; the life of my
life thou art.

Yet if man and brute deny me, if Nature spurn me
back,
If Grace deflect her channels, bear witness, thou
starry track!

I know in my heart of hearts the hills that can still
be trod ;
I will take up my heart in my hands, and go up
alone to God—
I come to Thee last, but I come ; they fail'd me in
all the strife—
Those signs of help and comfort ; here is the end
of my life.
I find no refuge but Thee, O last and first in the
wide
And empty worlds of the soul ; Thou canst not
cast me aside !

Yet hearts which are offer'd to anything under the
sun
Are not for long rejected, at least by Nature for one ;
And though the hands which are wise, high gifts
may hold for a space,
We are not defrauded long of all communion with
Grace ;
Man never truly waited, if man could ease him a
smart ;
The rudest beast of the field responds to the human
heart ;
While those who cry, "O, my darling !" with great
hearts inly stirr'd,
Are little less than the angels—that is my gospel
word !

INSUFFICIENCY

VEILS OF ISIS

NATURE is naked until man's own mind
Has rainbow hues to all her form assign'd;
  And she in turn provides his garments dim:
Say, who shall robe her when his hands unbind,
  Who unclothe him?

INSUFFICIENCY

THOU, having seen it, art thou satisfied?—
That platform of the morning bulges wide
Above the purple gorges, in the dim
Exalted light. Far down the sea-mews swim,
Far down the breakers on the crags expend
Their strength in gulfs where never men descend;
And thou, awhile from sea and shore aloof,
Art as one issued on a palace roof
In Esclair-Monde, from its exalted tiers
Gazing serenely down on moving spheres,

And far above the night's enfolding arch
Beholding systems in their stately march,
With dark, dead stars lamenting as they glide :—
Say, having seen this, art thou satisfied ?

Alas, the halting accents of thy speech,
Can scarce another thine experience teach,
Nor can thy brain, by wonders overwrought,
Shape as thou wouldst the higher course of thought,
Since in reflection's hush do thoughts most come !
So pass the moods of ecstasy to some
More sadden'd state, which knows not throne or
crown,
And at the last thou goest slowly down,
With weaker steps, along the arduous slope,
Somewhat disorder'd with thy former hope—
A little dazed—but conscious on the whole
That these high places cannot fill the soul ;
That Nature's peaks, which few before have trod,
Do not specifically lead to God,
And are not therefore of the soul's concern.
Only when recollections shall return
In after hours, the soul may then look back,
From quiet ways, up the precipitous track,
Where saffron morning o'er the sea spreads fair ;
And know that the soul's ends are everywhere.

A CONFIDENCE

THAT which you seek for in your heart of hearts—
That which transcends both Nature and the Arts—
Great beyond conscious grasp of human mind,
But ever as the rest and goal
Acknowledged by your secret soul—
Brother, I promise, you shall surely find.

And if you ask me—knowing it so great—
The solid ground on which I dare to state
That you shall certainly attain at length;
Learn that beyond the things which seem
I have divined your dream,
And also know your hidden source of strength.

Have courage, therefore! Keep your daily road,
And after your own individual mode
Do that which comes to hand, but well and true;
For failures sometimes made—as such—
Be not concern'd too much;
Fear not yourself—I have no fear for you.

STRANGE HOUSES OF SLEEP

HOW IT IS ATTAINED IN THE SUNSET

Now this is true philosophy, that sense
Is sometimes held in such a high suspense
As if a man's feet taken from the ground—
The world beneath him spinning round and round—
He finds, at length permitted to descend,
All old, familiar scenes at some far end,
And where the runnel by his thatch should be
Hears the loud roar of a discordant sea.

Of such suspension hear a little space—
That which bechanced me in an hour of grace,
When the time-limits fixing life and thought,
Like landmarks storm-effaced, to nothing brought,
Permit that in the circle of a dream
There slips, unnoticed by, a century's scheme,
Or, twixt the lark's last note and swift descent,
That years of rapture to the soul are lent.

It fell upon an eve made rich with heat
Of spikenard odours and frankincense sweet
Which the deep-breathing earth gave forth from
    her—
ITEM—an ecstasy of nard and myrrh—

HOW IT IS ATTAINED AT SUNSET

That a fair haunt which in the woods I trod
Turn'd on a sudden to a church of God,
And down the path, as down an aisle, I pass'd
Through umbrage issuing to light at last;
An hundred feet above the plain a crest
Attain'd, confronted by the burning West.

Scarlet and gold, how vividly, had met,
And deeps beyond all deeps of violet
Open'd behind; above was snowy fleece
Of stainless vapour: glory, one with peace,
Was blazon'd there. The heart of solar fire
Outdrew me by ineffable desire,
Till it flash'd on me, with o'ermastering force,
That I was native to the starry course,
And that the peace of God surpassing speech
Through the light only could my spirit reach.
Deep, deep, I gazed, till deeps within me yearn'd;
Deep, till that light to other splendours turn'd;
Deep, till those splendours to a point drew in,
And the eye's sense alone I lived within—
Lived, from the flesh set free, the soul upcaught
Far past the heaven of stars, the heaven of thought.
And the soul died, but something greater still
Leap'd flame-like into me, her place to fill;
I was keen spirit, from the soul made free,
Which is, which hath been and through all will be,
And then once more I was an eye which sees
Into unutterable mysteries;

While undiffused, yet limitless, thereon
The searching point of naked splendour shone,
A dreadful rapture rending through and through—
As I was known therein, I also knew.
Yes, in the light, I knew, with all made one
By the same law which poises star and sun;
For moving systems marks a single track;
Which sends forth pilgrim souls and draws them
back;
From out of One the multiple evolves
And then the many in the One dissolves,
That when the end which is no end befall
Nothing be lost, but God be all in all.

Out of all time, in that great day's decline,
All love, all knowledge, for a space were mine,—
But holy words are wanting to declare;
And at the fine thereof returning where—
Five hundred feet above the plain—a crest
I found confronted by the burning West:
Lo, scarlet—gold—how vividly!—had met
And deeps beyond all deeps of violet,
While sinking in the lowland at my feet
The lark his brown wings hid in meadow-sweet.

PLUMES OF SABLE

WASTE, waste, waste,—but the voice in the waste
of the sea!
The dread, sheer height of a hopeless night! And
the heart—Ah, the heart in me!
I know where the wild is wider, I know of a peak
more dread—
O the waste and the height of the heart when the
star from the heart has fled!

THE INTERLOCUTORY DISCOURSE

FORTH on our quest some years agone we set:
How fares it with us? If the end is yet,
Or if we still must follow otherwhere,
Straightway in brief to each let each declare.
For me I pause a moment on the road
To mark how far is still the heart's abode.

STRANGE HOUSES OF SLEEP

As one towards morning tide a dream recalls
While heavy sleep as yet his sense enthrals,
I look on those long spaces over past,
And forward, dreaming if the trance will last.
While round me move the deeper dreamers here.
Perchance for us the waking time is near
Since one advantage over these have we,
Who know how sleep expands her sorcery,
While others in their spell such comfort take
As comes to those who hold they truly wake.
Perchance we thought it from the first — who knows?
When that awoke to trouble our repose,
That grand debate which did the quest begin—
Life, and the ways of life, and how therein
Best might ambition and its force applied
Insure our getting on before we died.
In either case, whate'er the cost or pain,
Resolved were we to triumph, to attain;
And yet despite this effort of the will
Much, it would seem, remains to tax our skill...
Set forth the subject as we view'd it then—
That life one duty has imposed on men:—
How to get on—the lesson all must learn;
By open ways if possible to earn
Their high success, if not by ways unknown.
All ends worth seeking, say, from star to stone,
We pass'd in thought before us, ere our choice
Was made; but those which common hearts rejoice

Seem'd scarcely worth life's dedicated span,
Nor did some greater aims pursued by man
Seem likely to avail him in the end :—
Such signal triumphs as on art attend ;
Such crowns in paths of knowledge seized at times ;
The laurel wreaths of rhymers and their rhymes ;
Devotion's guerdon for a country's weal ;
Due praise we gave them, owning their appeal,
But did with blessing true their claim dismiss.
Full long we ponder'd, weighing that with this,
Nor did the lower walks of life disdain ;
But in the end we found that trades were vain,
And all the crowded ways where men compete ;
That e'en the daily bread which all must eat
'Twere better, if it might be, to forego
Than daily bread for our sole object know ;
That wealth and luxury and social place
And seats among the mighty of the race
May in themselves be honourable things,
But insufficient for ambition's wings.
How, therefore, truly to get on ? said we ;
Then paused a moment, since it seem'd to be
No small achievement that, with hearts content,
We could from public interests dissent
And from all competitions stand aside.
But presently we found that ere he died
The common man saw vanity in these,
And now, as then, the saint their contact flees.
What true end, therefore, over and before
All these remains ?—O knowledge, evermore

Follow'd and worshipp'd! O ye lights of mind!
Ye secrets of the deeps all deeps behind!
Ye hidden forces! Man—his height, his deep—
Ways of the waking world and world asleep—
Praise we invoked on all who these pursued;
For us we left them to their solitude:
How therefore truly to get on? we said.
And so it came to pass our souls were fed
With the great notion of a path untrod
When something told us that our end was God.
Whereat we blest, as paths already tried,
The grand old faiths, but put their claims aside,
And forth upon our varied ways we went,
What weary days, on God's attainment bent!
Of many men did you perchance inquire,
To saint and sage spurr'd on by one desire,
And over all the world did learn of all.
But whatsoever did your days befall,
The circle of that world has brought you round
Unto the starting point—and how much found?
How much, how little? . . . I inquired of none—
Of One alone by One to seek the One
For me at least avail'd. Withdrawn in mind
By blessed contemplation's ruling kind,
From sleep of midnight unto sleep of dawn
I sought the vision out of both withdrawn;
And me the circle of the deeps has brought
Back to the starting point—but how much taught?
Leastways one lesson both for me and you—
Ours is the way of the attainment true;

GROUNDS OF UNION

No better end than that we two divine
Has shone upon your pathway or on mine,
All paths attempting where all lights have shone,
And ours the only way for getting on.
So forward, therefore; somewhere lurks the end:
All in good time—His time—that's best, my
friend!

GROUNDS OF UNION

THERE is no need to take thy hand,
To touch thy lips, or thee to greet;
Nor must I say in what far land,
Out of all time, we first did meet;
As in this russet hour we stand,
That which has parted us meseems
A curtain in some House of Dreams.

Or, in this aching scheme of things,
If memories like these delude,
My yearning towards thee, taking wings,
Doth ever in the past intrude;
From such dim halls thy picture brings,
And since it sees thee everywhere
Can skry no world but thou art there.

STRANGE HOUSES OF SLEEP

I will not speak of love to thee,
  For, having look'd in eyes like thine,
Past love's inscrutable mystery,
  Something more sacred, more divine
And undeclared than love I see;
    And what those secret depths enfold,
    That, in my heart, for thee I hold.

Taught in strange schools, this earthly place
  Finds task-work in my forms of speech;
But, looking on thy chasten'd face,
  All hast thou learn'd which I would teach:
By thy tired eyes and tortured grace,
    Surely when forming thee God sigh'd—
    Thou art so wan, so mortified.

From us, whom Nature never knew,
  That common health is far removed
Whereof old saints, with instinct true
  But angel-mildness, disapproved:
They read our weakness through and through,
    Saw that strong thews and nerves of earth
    Win hardly towards the second birth.

The knots which bind our souls are such
  As earthly ties would strain and start;
Each would not hold in each so much,
  If ill-content on earth to part:
That once the ways we walk should touch
    For consolation, not for need,
    That which is merciful decreed.

THEOPHANY

Let then those ways divide, not they
  Either conjoin or disconnect:
Thou wilt not fail me on a day,
  Nor I from they sheer height deflect
By stooping towards thy house of clay;
    But when that day for thee and me
    Comes, at the end, remember me!

In the great session, when They meet
  For rites of union, thou wilt wait,
Knowing I follow on thy feet,
  And I will pause, if thou be late,
A little at the mercy-seat;
    Till God shall make us one in Him,
    Hide under wings of seraphim.

THEOPHANY

Too long unmindful of the great concern,
We did from errors of our way return,
From strange side issues and from paths involved.
Thenceforth on reasonable life resolved,
Our sins fell from us, and unloosed with these
Were many morganatic marriages,
Incurr'd regardless of the sacred things
Which life imposes on the sons of Kings
Who wait for restoration to their own,
Since old mischance deprived of crown and throne.

Full many ways we tried in vain since then,
Nor did forsake the common paths of men
Uncertain of the ends to which they lead—
Wherein is little for the greater need
Which on the sons of Kings full sadly falls,
Hearing their former country's far off calls.

But set with steadfast feet in these new ways,
What quest might glorify our later days
Whose hearts so high are fix'd on things above?
Ah, friends! Regarding thus the place of love,
What could we seek herein to hear or see
But the sweet rumours of its mystery?
Of Him who shall at length our crown restore
Some faint reflections on this earthly shore?

And so it fell that from the dream we kept
Within our hearts, a flame of ardour leapt,
Till we, drawn forth to seek in every place
The tidings of His presence and their grace,
Did in the end, by golden legends led,
A realm of mystery and wonder tread,
Chosen from all the places of the earth
To see God manifest by human birth.

Kings which had follow'd, from their realms afar,
The age-long portent of a certain star;
Priests of a line which since the world began
Was set to offer sacrifice for man;

THEOPHANY

And, far across the melancholy seas,
The silent keepers of the mysteries;
Met in their crowds upon that haunted ground—
And we, the king's sons, waiting to be crown'd.

But not alone the royal and the wise,
And pontiffs with illuminated eyes,
Or those who, secretly instructed, knew
How old traditions won fulfilment true;
There also came the shepherds from the hills,
And he who sows the ground and he who tills.
From noisy marts the merchant came in haste;
Came too, the lawless rovers of the waste;
And from the city came the child of sin;
To see God born and a new life begin
To make refreshment in a weary world.

So round about the holy place were furl'd
The nations' banners; peace on nations fell,
And the long strife of creeds was ended well.
The spirit of the world its pride gave up,
And kiss'd the hallows and the holy cup;
The flesh dissolving utter'd as it died
The sacred mass words, and was purified;
And Lucifer, the Prince, who knelt with them,
Turn'd sweetly praying towards Jerusalem.

So thus it fell, upon a certain morn,
All in the hearts of men, that God was born,
And that we also knew what sacred things
Such birth imposes on the sons of Kings.

STRANGE HOUSES OF SLEEP

OF FAITH AND VISION

THE light of life, the light which dwells in life,
With perfect, free and undivided love,
We seers have loved for ever; have abode
In any conscious gloom of heart or mind
Unwillingly; have ever into day,
With strife and clamour of aspiration, sprung;
And when we found true sunlight we were blest.
We have not scorn'd the simpler gifts of faith,
Yet sought in knowledge and the soul's clear sight
That lucid world, all scatter'd beams of thought
Receiving and reflecting; but when those
Were granted not, we held to faith and hope;
And any ray diffused along the dark,
Though less than nothing to the world at large,
Our hearts collected, cherish'd, dwelt therein,
And bless'd the Giver; counting all things well;
As grateful for His silence as His speech;
Keeping His silence with the same brave heart
Which, bidden, would have trumpeted His word;
For ever waiting on that word by Him
Withheld for ever. . . . To the end of all
Approaching now, we fail but do not faint:
He has not seal'd our mission or granted us

The consolation of His messengers.
We have not heard His voice; we have not work'd
His miracles, nor stood before His world
And testified that we indeed were sent;
But we have loved the light, and here and now,
Before the antechamber of the tomb
And underneath the quiet wings of death,
Faith helps us still amidst true calm of soul
To say: The quest is broken for a while,
But ended not; and, whether life or death,
We still desire the vision and the truth.
Bid therefore, Lord, thy servants pass in peace
Beholding thy salvation with their eyes!

THE PATH

SEEING that all which lives beneath the sun
Is, in the last resource, explain'd by One;
That every will which works or star which sings
In fine goes back into the font of things;
That by a final gathering of force
The soul of man shall, to complete its course,
With a great rush return from whence it came;
The last and first can differ but in name,
And there is one beginning and one end.
How then these varied interests defend

Which now distract and dissipate the soul,
Leading it daily further from the whole
Wherein we know there lies our only good?
Ah, we have heard and have not understood!
From the confessions of our lips the heart,
Untouch'd and unconvinced, has stood apart,
So that mere words have trick'd us over long.
But, when the soul is search'd, the soul proves strong;
Zenith and Nadir and the Sacred Hill,
Show nothing keener than the human will,
Directed wisely unto wisdom's term.
Let us be therefore bold, and here affirm
That one strong wrench and that alone man needs
To set himself apart from evil deeds;
And if in ceasing utterly from these
The true Path lies, then are all mysteries
So well within the circle of his days
That if in truth there sounds a seraph's praise
About the white light of a central throne,
Not to the end shall angels serve alone.
Man's voice with theirs may join, he stand with them,
Nor fail at last of any diadem
Which can crown souls in any place unknown,
Or—if the stars have thrones—lose star and throne.

All this, however, is but mystic speech—
Our lip-confessions show what man must reach;
The soul its origin from One discerns,
And the soul's rest is when the soul returns.

THE PATH

But up that steep incline which once we trod,
When we came down—we know not why—from
God,
We also know that none to climb begin,
Nor dare until they cast away their sin.

Now, is it hard for man to sin no more?
To say that all which drew aside before
Henceforth for him is of its lure bereft,
That to go upward is the one course left?
Bear with me, friends, if what I know full well,
Of all evasions free, for once I tell:
This is not hard to any heart resolved,
Since in the soul's bent is one change involved,
One simple reconstruction of the will;
Then from the soul shall pass the lust of ill.

Think that outside our end all toil is vain;
Think that who wills can to the end attain;
Know that what does not to that end belong
Is folly always when it is not wrong;
Fix this before you, and you shall not err;
Nothing shall tempt you, nothing shall deter.
These are plain words, but their high sense enrings
The solemn secret of acquiring wings,
And from a complex to a simple mode
Can bring the soul, so that it knows the road;
So, seal'd with all simplicity, discerns
How what was many to the One returns.

VALE

Good-night; the hour is late, the house is cold,
The fires have smoulder'd down, the lamps are spent,
And all the visitors that came and went,
Sleep—which I also need—doth now enfold.
Late, late it grows—how long before we meet—
Beyond the fells, the fastness, the abyss?
O ways too far for over-weary feet!
O heart uncertain, where no goal there is!
Somehow, somewhere, in darkness or rich gleam
Yet shall we meet! Till then—good night, sweet dream!

PART II

THE HIDDEN SACRAMENT OF THE HOLY GRAAL

N.B.—The initial design of this Mystery Play is referable to a friend and fellow-worker in the mysteries, who, for the present, remains anonymous. The collaboration also embraces a portion of the text, but outside the archaic touch which is occasionally common to each, it is thought that the respective shares will be readily allocated to their proper writers in virtue of a certain distinction of style.

THE HOLY GRAAL

THE
PERFECT MYSTERY AND SEMBLANCE OF THE HOLY GRAAL

AND OF THOSE THAT SERVE THEREOF

SCENE.—*The lower portion of the stage, representing the World, either hung with tapestries or curtains, or else set with wood flats. Sufficient lighting for audience to distinguish features and no more.*— R.I.E. *Mediæval Table, with chairs or benches.*

UP STAGE.—*The Temple of the Graal, which should be circular in shape, having a vaulted roof painted sapphire colour, and emblazoned with the Sun, Moon and Stars. In the centre, the Shrine which, if permissible, should be an altar, but otherwise a mediæval market-cross, having in the midst thereof the Graal Cup, of the appearance of Emerald-coloured jasper, glowing red within and enriched by a stand after the manner of chased gold. The back-cloth, a reproduction of a mediæval landscape, with the hill-castle of Mont Salvatch in the far distance. All lights full.*

On the rise of the curtain, discovered before the Shrine the THREE KEEPERS OF THE GRAAL :

—One, in the centre, is an ancient man in the vestments of a BISHOP; *of the others, the one on the right hand is of middle life and the third, on the left hand, a beardless youth: both are in priestly vestments. They are surrounded, in addition to the Torchbearers, by the Seven Deacons of the Graal, clothed as* equites clerici, *that is, with a cassock descending to the feet, a surplice of white linen, a knightly mantle broidered with violet, a ruby pectoral cross, a girdle of violet silk knotted in front. The* CHIEF DEACON *stands behind the* BISHOP, *and has the six other Deacons, three on each side.*

The BISHOP *offers incense in a thurible. . . . The* BISHOP *sets down the thurible, and turns to the Chief Deacon and Brethren.*

BISHOP

Veni ad me, fratres carissimi, accipite osculum sanctæ fraternitatis et verbum pacis et transeant a me inter vos omnes.

He gives the Kiss of Peace to the SECOND KEEPER *of the* GRAAL, *from whom it passes to the* THIRD KEEPER *and thence to the* CHIEF DEACON *and the rest of the Brethren. Lights off. A dark curtain falls from* A *to* A. *Enter,* L.U.E., MASTER, *with seven Scholars to* C.

THE HOLY GRAAL

The Master

Now that a transitory place of stay
Our toilsome journey finds, before we know
What further travail fills the toilsome way,
I bid you, good my sons, to tell this day
How ye believe poor man fares here below:
Let each in turn the cause and order shew,
As seems to him, of our most grievous stress,
And how it is that in such weariness
This life is spent. For some the ample store
Of gold and lands will blame that life is sore;
Others declare that bitter poverty
The most torments our days with misery;
While gloomy preachers oft of death will prate
Which reaps alike the high and mean estate
And leaves no bliss at all or consolation,
But all that lives brings quickly to vexation.
The sick man says: If I were quick and able,
I would not murmur at my chance unstable.
He that is whole and fain his fill to eat
Bewails his fate because he finds no meat.
Some hold that lowly men are ever grieved,
Yet he that in a king's house was conceived
Will make lament, crying: Alas, on high
I am but set foul evil to descry!
So one that as a hermit dwells alone
Will, doubt not, for his solitude make moan,

And still another at his chance will weep
Who all his days in fellowship must keep.
Wherefore, my scholars, on your faith declare
Which is the greatest cause of human care.

FIRST SCHOLAR

Sir, can you doubt what dread it is
Which turns all mortal things amiss?
For, whether poor or wealthy, death
Daunts every heart, while hearts draw breath;
And though a man with dance and play,
In all fair guise, keeps holiday,
One at his lintel still will stand,
And closer than his own right hand
Will keep for ever by his side.
If man be strong or man be weak,
Sir Death shall not be far to seek.
Surely, therefrom he shall not hide:
In all the world there is no art
To heal him of that fatal dart.

SECOND SCHOLAR

Not with my brother is my mind,
For joy in death the best Knights find,
And even seek it spear in hand.
Therefore I may not understand
How some should thus fell dangers brave
If yet their greatest ill in death they have.
But I would say that man is most oppress'd

With grief while his felicity and rest
He looks to find in goods and earthly stuff,
Since of such matters none may gain enough,
But ever toil their barren heaps to swell:
In servage foul, condemn'd with stores to dwell
That are but gold-a-dreams and faerie,
Having no substance true nor mastery
To help them aught. And so a poor villein
Man lives with sweat of brow and sorry strain
Of his sad labour, till all toil has end—
What time good death comes forth and proves his
friend.

THIRD SCHOLAR

Sir, there are many that with wealth do good,
So I am fain to swear by Holy Rood
That man in penury is sore aggrieved
And having little is of that bereaved.
Behold how high Lords eat up his estate,
His goods despoiling for their garners great!
Surely of all things baneful this is worst,
That one should go with hunger and with thirst
Through all his mortal days companionèd.
He fares, to wrack and wrath of storm exposed,
Is least with these to strive by shields disposed,
In sorry rags by day apparellèd,
While straw provides at night a cheerless bed.
Nor does for this his life in idlesse pass,
Since toil that in green youth his guerdon was
Fills up the measure of futurity,

And little gain hath he of all his days;
Nor in his passing wins he greater praise,
But in contempt sinking him down to die,
He finds in death more deep obscurity;
Nor in such sorry life is better taught
To meet his end; nor goes he less to naught;
Nor can more firmly look than other some
Towards holy bliss which may hereafter come.
  On such good grounds I hold the poor man's ill
More great than his who keeps of goods a fill.

Fourth Scholar

Now if a man be sick, it is right sure
That he can find no joy while pains endure;
But if he hold his road with strength and health,
It follows haply he shall come to wealth;
And if he fail therein, his poor estate
Drags not so long a chain or grievous weight
As those whom fell mal ease all rest denies,
Whatever comfort may from goods arise.

Fifth Scholar

He that will ever fare forth all alone
Comes to his journey's end with many a moan,
As many faithful histories relate;
And did the highest guerdon on him wait,
Wretched is he withal, if there
Be none his prize to share.

THE HOLY GRAAL

Sixth Scholar

So wretched thrice who, sharing all with one
Or many, finds himself thereby undone.
He that will compass him with many a friend
Most certainly from foes shall have his end.

Seventh Scholar

Full tender am I of my age,
Nor can in great debates engage
Or thoughts with wit of words proclaim;
But if, in fine, I dared to name
My heart's device, this should I tell—
That none among you reason well;
For neither death with its sharp sting
Nor penury to woe can bring.
As one maintains, the stout of heart
With jollity to death depart;
Poor men receive their share of joy;
Some rich Lords live without annoy;
The sick man hopes with time to mend;
He that is whole a jocund road may wend;
And so for ever in each hard estate
There is some joy not all disconsolate.
Nathless, you truly say, this life is maul,
So, if you would that I should publish all,
I will deliver that which I intend:
Sirs, I believe that here is the true end

Why man is sorry in this hapless sphere;—
Not for the chance of death, or other fear,
Not for the sorrow that on him may fall;
But, heed ye well; the answer of it all
Is secret lore and master-craft most high,
Reserved and hidden in a mystery.
Now, know ye well, within this world is fix'd
One treasure only and one joy unmix'd,
One rich delight, one peace without an end,
One healing salve which can all hurts amend,
One holy house where foes can never reach—
More of this hidden matter ask me not to teach!

The Master

Ex ore infantum was said of old;
Herein the very truth is haply told;
And he who lights upon this secret store
Shall know that all his days were loss before.
Nathless, I doubt if in life's lower ground
Has purblind man the place of wonder found,
However much his halting steps bestir.
'Tis true some tell us of enchanted Vr,
Built out of sight deep in the morning land;
And some there are whom none can understand
Which, as they say, have visited in dream
The moving palace that they call Irêm;
While other some with fever in their blood
Do rave of marvels they have seen in Hud.
To make an end, the healing salve—I say—
Shall bless the heart which finds it on a day.

THE HOLY GRAAL

FIRST SCHOLAR

It well appears that none such joy can gain.

SECOND SCHOLAR

Shall man seek for it in some uncouth land?

THIRD SCHOLAR

Is it beheld with eye and grasp'd with hand?

FOURTH SCHOLAR

Does it fall down from heaven as summer rain?

FIFTH SCHOLAR

Sirs, for this treasure-trove I am not fain:
I deem it fond device and gramarye;
For all such guises it misliketh me.

SIXTH SCHOLAR

And so say I, *per Corpus Domini!*

THE MASTER

You are misguided all, by Holy Rood,
And have not this great matter understood,
Because your eyes are blinded by false wit;
Most certainly you shall not light on it!
Myself in other days did joys conceive
Of quests like this, and in my heart believe
That, for his spirit's and his life's defence,
A man might haply find the quintessence,

Since very surely, as the sages shew,
Thesaurus latet in Mercurio ;
Yes, if a man could see them with his eyes,
Sulphur and salt do hold great mysteries,
While he which can extract the seed of gold
The wealth of all this world shall truly hold.
But haste we now to reach our journey's end,
And may good angels on our path attend !
Thus shall we gain if not all term of quest,
Yet so a little of the mind its rest,
With ease of body and no greater blame
Than souls may have which shall escape the flame
That cleanses sin in purgatory's well,
Having been ransom'd first from fiends of hell.
From magic arts, meanwhile, and witchcraft may
St. Mary shield our paths on every day !
So God shall save us and bring judgment quick
Less on the sinner than the heretic.
May Plato's method ne'er prevail with us—
To all such whimsies, *phi Diabolus !*
And may our steps keep straight within the schools
Confessing only Aristotle's rules !
Haste therefore, now cool vesper wafts afar
The splendid fervours of the day's bright star !

THE YOUNG SCHOLAR

Sir, by your leave, it may not be ;
This is no journey now for me,
To whom all lore of schools is naught
Since there has come into my thought

A certain word that I shall tarry
Here in this place, though all miscarry.

FIRST SCHOLAR

Then keep the devil's holiday! [*Exit* R.U.E.

SECOND SCHOLAR

Delirat ille, so I say! [*Exit* R.U.E.

THIRD SCHOLAR

Belial and Bel beset your way! [*Exit* R.U.E.

FOURTH SCHOLAR

Here you shall lack not elf and fay,
Black goat, or wizard's Sabbath play.
[*Exit* R.U.E.

FIFTH SCHOLAR

Speed you, fair sir; all saints, I pray,
Stand round you, lest your steps should stray;
Nor let the arch-fiend's foul array
And Ashtaroth your soul bewray! [*Exit* R.U.E.

SIXTH SCHOLAR

In hell's foul pit shall be your stay! [*Exit* R.U.E.

THE MASTER

Ah, fair my son, God give you grace—
Since I must leave you in this place! [*Exit* R.U.E.

THE HIDDEN CHORUS

From arrow flying in the light,
From demon wiles which lurk at noon
And things unclean that move at night
In stealthy mist beneath the moon,
God save and have you—waking, sleeping—
Ex hoc nunc, in His holy keeping!

The YOUNG SCHOLAR *is left alone*, C., *standing with bowed head till the laughter of the Six Companion Scholars dies away in the distance. He then gazes about him with something of dismay in his aspect.*

YOUNG SCHOLAR

Now am I left in this dim place alone,
My Master and my friends from me have gone—
Gone too the secret words, which all unsought
Were in the hours of dream and darkness taught,
Even to one forlorn, by him who came
Withholding his true place and name,
But things so high announcing that, meseems,
This earth henceforth is thinnest woof of dreams.
Yet sometimes in my thought a gate I find
Through which a man may leave the dream behind

And in a little while all true things reach.
Ah, my true Master, now thy faithful speech
I lack indeed, thus casting schools aside
And standing sadly where the ways divide,
Full little knowing of the path I take!
O thou who didst my life from dreams awake
And to be mindful of my want
Didst strangely covenant,
Be with me here, I plead,
In this my great disquietude and need! [*A pause.*
Alas, no help is mine in this strange land
Where doubtful shapes do lurk on either hand!
Where shall I turn, whither my journey be?
For now I fear the powers of Faerie,
The hollow world where Pan is emperor,
That world where many a soul lies stricken sore,
There in thick darkness Doomsday to abide,
Sol close by Venus Queen and Helen's side,
With all false Gods that ruled the deeps of old
And fiends that the False Angel's face behold.
Of sacraments unclean they there partake,
And with the wine of death their thirst they slake.
Ah, woe is me! And whither shall I go?
How shall I pass from this dark world of wo?
From such a maze profound as long before
Was set for that accursèd Minotaur?
Too soon I come unto a high debate,
Nor know at all how I can mend my state;
Yet well I deem that, closer unto me
Than eye to eye, lies heal'd the magistry

Which can the whole world change to angel gold
And make poor man to taste of bliss untold.
Yea, surely here mine eye should this behold
But that my body faints with weariness
Of the long journey and the fell distress
That falls on footsore men which have no meat.
Lo! I am gone: no strength is in my feet
And my cold heart grows still within my breast:
Here is my grave, and here my body's rest.

[*Fainting, sinks on ground.*

Within, song and laughter. Enter, R.I.E., *company of drinkers, who stand about the table, cup in hand.*

SONG

He shall not thrive whose cup is dry:
So say we all, and so say I.
There was a man in Babylon
That made his house out of a tun;
And he was wise, and so say I.
There was a wife in Ermony
That had two husbands, certainly;
And one was wine, all red to see;
And she was wise, and so say I:
He is a fool whose cup is dry.
There was a maid that journey'd far,
For she set forth and found a star;
That star shines full in fair old wine:
The best of it to thee and thine!
But she was wise, and so say I;
He shall not thrive whose cup is dry.

THE HOLY GRAAL

PRIMUS COMPOTATOR

Companions, to my tale give ear,
For I am call'd the Mariner
And have sail'd forth both far and near!

SECUNDUS

Ben'dicite! But by the mass
Here is a lie that shall not pass,
Since I trow well you have not been
Above a league from churchtown green!

TERTIUS

Beshrew me, this is John-a-Noakes;
His legs have marr'd the parish stocks!

PRIMUS

Now, by my faith, you read askew!
Strange countries have I wander'd through;
In outland cities I have been
And monstrous marvels there have seen;
Seas have I pass'd that are not told
In charts and books by men of old:
Thus am I call'd the Mariner,
And, wit you well, my ship is here!

[*Lifting up cup and drinking.*

But who is this upon the ground?
[*Going to Scholar.*
Gossips, this man is in a swound!
God save you well, what chance is this?
[*Raising Scholar.*

SCHOLAR (*murmuring*)

Alas, my end is near, I wis,
And these are visions that I see—
False shapes of dying fantasy!

COMPOTATOR

Alack! poor man, hereof partake,
Meet not alone all thirst to slake,
But with such strength thy heart endue
That thou no more shalt grieve or rue!

SCHOLAR (*drinking*)

Thou sayest well; but tell me where
That cup is hid which shines most fair—
The cup of mighty orison
Which once beholding, there is none
That is not fill'd with benison.

COMPOTATOR

His eyes are wild, his face is wan.
It chills my heart to look thereon.

THE HOLY GRAAL

SCHOLAR

I pray you, each and every one,
Shew me the house of high intent
And light of vision never spent;
Where never fadeth the high day;
Where quickening wine is ever pour'd;
Where the bright feast shines on the board;
Where they that sit are well content
And count this world foul banishment.

COMPOTATOR

(*To others*) With Gramarye his wit is mazed.
Sir, give you grace, for, God be praised,
Here shall be found all joy you seek
When you drink with me, jowl by cheek!

[*Leading* SCHOLAR *to table*, R.I.E. SCHOLAR *looks about him in confusion and sinks into chair.* COMPOTATOR *fills and gives him a great cup of wine, which he drinks. He then starts up.*

SCHOLAR

Grammercy for your courteousness
To one, *pardie*, in sore distress,
Alike diseased in heart and head
And less among the quick than dead!
For lying prone, I dream'd a dream
Which made man's life mere glamour seem;

Lo, sure I thought that in this place
There should come freely such high grace,
That I should no more grieve or fear!
Yea, in my frenzy I saw near,
A jasper cup which hands unseen,
Exalted heaven's bright gates between,
Until beyond the pole's clear star
It shone with ruddy light afar.
Thereafter, loosed from mortal things,
As one abruptly finding wings,
Within that cup I dwelt, and knew
All heaven's keen rapture through and through.
But now meseems that this is nought
And deep in dream alone I wrought.

COMPOTATOR

Sir, you say well: believe me, this
Is earth's one true and only bliss! [*Drinking*.
That wine is red and fair to hold
True wisdom writes with style of gold,
And in one doctrine seeks to dwell—
That he lies well who has drunk well.

SCHOLAR

But if a man has toped good store?

COMPOTATOR

Then wisdom finds one maxim more:
To fill the cup and drink yet more.

THE HOLY GRAAL

SCHOLAR

Tu es rex Philosophiæ;
And hence I count it a fair day
When in this place I went astray:
For here I learn that heaven's whole space
Is held within one cup of grace;

[*He lifts up the beaker.*

And they that otherwise do quest
Shall find no dwelling of the blest.
Then let the wine for ever red
Be canonised and worshippëd!
Here would I tarry all the year,
For summer glows unceasing here. [*Drinking.*

[*Meanwhile a solemn music begins to sound from without and the procession of the* GRAAL *passes slowly, with chanting, from* L. *to* R., *at the back of stage, amidst incense and light of torches. There is no manifestation of the sacred cup. The heads of the drinkers have sunk upon the board: only the* SCHOLAR *sees the procession. He shakes* COMPOTATOR PRIMUS *by the shoulder.*

SCHOLAR

Alas, alas, now am I all bejaped!
By sweet St. John, thou hast deceived me quite!
Awake, false fellow, from thy wits escaped!
Bestir thee, knave, or sore will I thee smite!

COMPOTATOR (*singing*)

There was a man in Babylon
That made his house out of a tun.

SCHOLAR

More bibb'd art thou than any loathly swine;
Thy wit is drown'd in heavy draughts of wine.
Awake thee, or I knock thy drowsy pate!
[*Again shaking him.*

COMPOTATOR

What is this matter, sir, you would debate?
Know you not this? When men have drunken well,
Then good sound sleep is fair and laudable.
Hence, trouble me no more, of courtesy,
For well quoth he that said, Let tosspots lie.

SCHOLAR

Thou dullard, wake, for I saw pass this road
A holy pageant of the bless'd abode,
Richly byseen in vestments every one,
And light about them such as fills that Sun,
Whereof the ancient men in Alchemy
Have sought long years to find the mastery!
It was full rare and glorious to behold:
I tell thee, fellow, that there is no gold
In all the earth so glorious and so bright;
'Twas fire that beareth life, and quickening light!

And all the while I heard such sweet descant
As songmen in high quires do use to chant:
Now well I know that with foul incantation
Thou hast bereft me of my true salvation.

COMPOTATOR

Alas! I see thou art by frenzy taken
As once before, when here outstretch'd forsaken;
Then didst thou babble of such matters vain
And dost to like distraction turn again.
I would, *pardie*, I might find hellebore,
Wherewith such wits as these were purged of yore!

SCHOLAR

Thou drunken man! With mine own eyes I view'd
This mystery of all high celsitude.

COMPOTATOR

I'll have no fellowship with men that rave:
God send thee quick deliverance to the grave!
Come, masters, hence; this scholar is full wood,
[*Rousing drinkers.*
And presently his knife shall let our blood.
[*Exit*, R.I.E., *singing.*

COMPOTATORES (*following*)

There was a man in Babylon
That made his house out of a tun.

SCHOLAR

Thus have I miss'd, by infamous device,
That mighty sacrament exceeding price
With which enspiritual powers amazed
My mortal eyes, when erst thereon they gazed;
But well I knew there swell'd such antiphon
As I would say they sing on Mount Syon;
[*Down stage.*
And as the high procession went its road
All Syon's peace upon the place abode. . . .
My soul is passing heavy and dismay'd! [*Kneeling.*
Ah, fair, sweet Lord, in heaven's glory array'd,
Forgive this sin whereof I now repent,
And look on him who is Thy penitent,
Assoiling me for Thy sweet passion's sake,
And of my fault bewail'd redemption make!
So shall my heart no more dark counsels hear,
Nor fiends most foul prevail, if Thou be near.
This grant me, Jesu, in Thy mercy dear!

As the SCHOLAR *rises, enter,* L.U.E., *a Young Man and a Girl, gaily dressed.*

JUVENIS

Listen, sweetheart, unto the nightingale,
Which now to the domed world sings such a tale
That changed by his decree are all things found,
Exalted by his mystery and crown'd.

THE HOLY GRAAL

Now is the sacring of Love's mass, the feast
Of that high god shewn forth to last and least
Of his true servants: now his priests assume
Their vestments; now his altar lights illume.
Incipit chorus: Lord of Love, arise!
And thus the Introit is intoned in solemn wise.
Kyrie eleison: Lord of Love, we pray
That thou have mercy on us for this day!
And then the *Gloria* chant they every one,
Giving to love all bliss and benison.
Credo in Deum Amoris next they sing,
The mighty God of Love thus honouring,
And so through secret halse and housel move
The sacred prodigies of holy Love,
Till this ineffable service thus is done.
There is no church nor quire of fair-wrought stone
That is with rich array so fair bysene;
For when the sun went down and mists gan rise,
After long glories at day's end, I ween,
These were the curtains of our sacrifice
That do enclose us from profane intent.
Then was the moon display'd to shine aloft
And be the lamp of this sweet sacrament;
The glowworms marshall'd bearing torches soft,
To serve before Love's altar well content;
And meadowsweet, which hath our sense enthrall'd,
Love's thurifer with good pretence is call'd;
While, as we hear, the nightingales in quire
Do sing the antiphon of our desire.

[*The* SCHOLAR *approaches them, listening.*

STRANGE HOUSES OF SLEEP

PUELLA

But tell me, sweet, I pray, what high reward
Waits those who serve with faith this sovereign Lord?

JUVENIS

Believe in this, there is no treasure found
But is the gift of him, our ruler crown'd,
And they that serve him rightly shall begin
Enough of rapture to discern therein,
For love is Lord of all and suzerain!
Earth's Kings bow down, acknowledging the reign
Above them each of this high emperor;
While clerks that would have wit must know his
lore,
Since without love clergy is foolishness
And all sinks down to pasture with distress.
Fair stores for building castles come to nought
And chantries meetly for petitions wrought,
If that strong god do not abide in each
And all the secret things of sweetness teach.
There shall be no bliss set in bower or hall,
Nor any joy shall follow on our call:
If we have goods they shall encompass woe;
If we would see, yet shall we nothing know;
If we would hear, dread noise shall only sound;
If touch, our flesh shall be in mortal swound;
If we would smell, it shall be hell's black smoke;
If we would taste, the act thereof shall choke.

But if with virtue and great steadfastness
We serve this god, he will for ever bless
And crown our days with great exuberance,
Keeping as still in his sweet maintenance.

SCHOLAR

It is most plain here is the thing I sought;
By this Knight's wisdom I must now be taught.
[*Turning to* JUVENIS.
Sir, you have spoken of Love's benison;
I pray you, tell me how such joy is won,
For hither am I come from a far land
The secret work of bliss to understand.
Save in this doctrine's great and hidden power
You shall instruct me well and warily,
No rapture shall I find at any hour;
And hence I ask you, of your charity,
That I may satiate my soul with good.

JUVENIS

So will I do forthwith, by Holy Rood!
Learn, firstly, that Love's service is full sweet;
His way is made most easy for your feet.
Him shall you worship not in toil and pain,
Nor do your suit with brows that sweat amain;
But if you be to his high paths inclined
Shall move therein with merriment of mind.
You shall not therefore in sad vesture ask
To wear his sweet yoke and perform his task,

But in gay robes be fittingly array'd.
To Bacchus next make pious sacrifice
Who is the master of all high device
And craft of love, whereby are men most blest!
Then furthermore, it is Love's high arrest
That from your heart you shall all dolour purge,
And with glad mien into his light emerge.
Your whole intent shall be to play and dance,
Singing full merrily, with great joyance;
And all your body hold in right accord,
If you be servant of this royal Lord. . . .
But now the sunset fires and fragrance call
To certain secret rites at even-fall;
Their wardens wait my advent. You, dear maid,
Shall your own bower seek out in this green glade
And deftly there your part prescribed fulfil:
Ere twilight tide shall turn to midnight still,
I look the shining of your eyes to greet
In guise for untold mysteries more meet.

[*Exit* R.U.E.

SCHOLAR

Alas for me! Now is my master gone:
Once more I stand forsaken and alone,
With none to help me in my bitter need.

PUELLA

But say not so, since I am here indeed;
He could but speak; I can do more than this,
And, if you trust to me, lead on to bliss.

THE HOLY GRAAL

Scholar

Art thou more wise than doctors in the schools?
Thou hast not ponder'd Aristotle's rules,
Still less at sovereign Plato's hidden spring
Demanded deeper wisdom's treasured thing.
Thy travail lies in song and psaltery
Rather, I wis, than in philosophy;
Of all fond crafts art thou the past mistress,
Of games and plays for pleasant idleness;
Yet, though thou art full tender of thine age,
Thou wouldst know more than any ancient sage.

Puella

Alas! fair sir, your wit is all askew:
You have mislearn'd that art which only counts for true.
For what is all the lore whereof you speak
But vain concerns for our poor heads too weak?
You would this world turn wholly upside down
And make new paradise within your crown.
You dream of things that here at least are not;
Of this and that, but all the best forgot;
Of visions seen at night; of shadow play;
Of suns at dusk and moons at high noonday.
You think that wit you have of ghostly sort,
Yet hide your eyes to look; you make report

How you have heard some voice with ear shut close,
And your own shadow mars your best repose.
Now tell me why you wander in this guise,
And I shall take you where your treasure lies!

SCHOLAR

Know therefore, maid, that in this place at hand
There is the treasure sought in every land:
Nearest of all things, yet of all most far,
On earth a lamp, in heaven yet shines a shining star;
A cup—a tree—its roots from dust do rise
And yet the branches shine in Paradise.
By all it is beheld, yet few can see;
To find it each man strives with right good will,
But on his deathbed is a seeker still.
If high or low, if rich or poor we be,
Still must we hold this matter in desire
And in the quest thereof shall never tire;
Yet is it order'd, though our rest be none
And not with life shall be our vigil done,
That with false shows we shall be aye mistaken
And of good counsel in our course forsaken.
For though this marvel come into our hand,
The shape of it we shall not understand:
Hence the fair treasure we shall look upon
But deem it nothing more than stock or stone;
Because since Father Adam did amiss
Before our eyes a heavy veil there is,
And we can win no sight of heaven's bliss,

Seeing the Lord, which is most sovereign
And high in Heaven's Light doth ever reign,
Has so ordain'd to be our punishment.
Behold as exiles hither are we sent,
And hence we pass unresting to and fro,
Yet nothing of this guerdon may we know,
Which is nathless no strange or fabled thing
Whereof in tales we hear the minstrels sing!
It boots us not to seek in journeys long
What is more close than singer and his song;
And if a man as priest shall serve God well
In offices and rites most laudable,
Holding the Faith, with mercy on the poor
And giving freely as God sendeth store,
Then certainly this Sangraal shall him pass
In holy quire and sacring of the Mass.
So if another prove him God's true Knight
And stoutly quit him for the kingdom's right,
He too shall hold the gift no emperor
Can ever count among his golden store;
And therefore men, where'er their course is run,
May gain this secret grace and benison;
Or at the least shall find its rule begin,
If the true light they harbour them within.

PUELLA

Such strange harangues for me no music make;
So, prithee, speak not any more of this,
Which nothing proves save idle talk, I wis!
Rather approach, your treasure find and take

Hid in mine eyes and body passing sweet;
With perfect bliss fulfill'd we then shall meet.
Come, love, and follow in my paths awhile,
That visions false may fade before my smile!
So fetously bedight and close at hand,
Within these woodland walks, my arbours stand
That in no tract is found retreat more fair
Or rigidly enclosed from all rude air
Of Aquilon aud surly Boreas,
And none but gentle winds about it pass.
There will I give you of such dainty meat
And delicates so rare will spread to eat,
That never king could feast in hall so well.
Heal'd shall we be therein from all dark spell,
Since I have herbs which those empower'd to taste
Forthwith in palaces of life are placed.
Those herbs, *pardie*, were gathered long ago
In hidden ways of lands that few men know!
Then come with me, if you be lief and dear,
And I will be your love for many a year!

SCHOLAR

Full oft, the Graal, with rites in secret heard,
Is by unspotted maidens minister'd,
And maids thereof alone can serve, I ween;
If you like them be privileged and clean,
I count our meeting bless'd in this my need;
And I will follow wheresoe'er you lead:
But if with secret guile to tempt you strive,
Then other ways shall save my soul alive.

THE HOLY GRAAL

PUELLA

Aroint thee, dunce in all sweet dalliance;
Here haunt alone the horrid darkness still,
And undisturb'd of silly dreams have fill;
While shapes more gruesome than the night advance
To work thy stupid head some unknown ill!
[*Exit* R.U.E.

SCHOLAR

Now am I left again in great distress,
With sinful souls to bear all heaviness;
True light denied about my steps or mind,
Meseems, I ne'er shall come this Graal to find,
Since here I see but shapes of great deceit,
Whence it meseems that I am judged unmeet
For that high quest and place of Paradise
Where the fair cup is shewn to mortal eyes.
[*Noise is heard from within.*
Alas! what further clamours now asise?

Enter, L.I.E., *a troop of Revellers, men and women, headed by a Fool. They dance round* SCHOLAR, C., *singing.*

CHORUS

A round, a round, a round!
The world of fools has folly crown'd.
There is no place for wisdom found;
King Fool unchallenged rules this ground,

To whose fair realm there is no bound :
His is the world ; the world is round—
A round, a round, a round !

The circle is broken into two groups, L. & R., *below* SCHOLAR, *and the* FOOL *stands to* L. *of* SCHOLAR.

FOOL

Let all men know, by my command,
That my sway spreads through every land,
From sea to sea and strand to strand.
There is no King nor Emperor,
No Judge, no Lord, nor Chancellor
But does me homage evermore.
I am set up and throned on high,
And as I look both far and nigh,
Behold the mad world passes by !
High lords in ermine robes array'd
At councils make a great tirade,
Yet by them is my power display'd.
I see rich men heap up their gold,
The poor in want wax grim and cold :
They all are sheep within my fold.
I see Tom Tosspot go his way ;
He keeps the maltworm's holiday,
And is my servant, by my fay !
True lovers all my livery wear ;
Motley it is, but light to bear ;
They carry it with jocund air.

The dance recommences more wildly, gathering about the SCHOLAR. *He is approached by the* FOOL *in his antics, who shakes his bells violently as the ring breaks up at length.*

FOOL

Young Master, prithee, of your grace,
Why wear such sad and sober face
When all kind folly loudly pleads
For modes and manners debonair?
Why also wear outlandish weeds,
As one but late from school escaped?
Mark these fair meads, so gaily draped;
Our motley mark and tousell'd hair!
Your heavy eyes, your careworn look
Do smack too much of wisdom's book.
I counsel you, let sense go hang
And join in time this clownish gang,
Which never learn'd to speak or spell
Aught save words delectable
In perfect praise of Folly's King;
And these with might and main they sing,
Nor care for wisdom's rule a fig,
But dance about and whirligig!

SCHOLAR

I pray you, sir, since now the hour is late
And on a pilgrimage from far I come,
Chide not the habit of my mean estate;
Perchance 'tis not more mean than other some!

I am a scholar and I seek as such
Some vestures of the mysteries to touch;
If Folly's themes and joys you folk prefer
I will not offer an affront to her,
Or counsel force on you her praise to cease;
Do you the same, and let us part in peace!

FOOL

His anxious face, outlandish vogue
And sorry accent well proclaim
This youth at best a cheerless rogue,
Unmeet to breathe kind Folly's name.
But, merry men, it matters not:
Come, leave him to his luckless lot;
And pipes and bells with jangling sound
Shall lead us to congenial ground—
Round and round, and merry go round!

[*The troop of Revellers make off*, R.I.E., *with shrill noises.*

SCHOLAR

The night is long which now is scarce begun;
Full sorely here the comfortable sun
I miss, who am so lowly and bewray'd:
Will no one come to offer me true aid?
Ah, Master good, thy prudent counsel left,
I am well visited, midst snares bereft!

THE HOLY GRAAL

The stage lightens, L.I.E., *and the Queen of Fairyland enters, habited in green samite, like a fair lady.*

QUEEN

Alas, poor youth, what sad mischance hath brought
Thy hapless steps to this sad place of thought,
Where verges of all worlds do mix and meet
And men are weariful of heart and feet?
In haste I pass along with clouded face,
Returning to my own auspicious place;
But all my powers have waned, my light is dim;
The haunting terror of a dubious hymn,
Which Nature never breathed through woodland trees,
Sounds in the cold air like the scourge of seas,
And restless things are moving to and fro,
To poison all the joy they cannot know.
In sooth the place with peril is beset;
But follow quickly, while the time is yet,
Where thou canst save at least thy flesh alive!

SCHOLAR

Ah, Lady fair, I would, I trow, derive,
Before my scanty days are overpast,
Some joy, long tides of sorrow to outlast,
And know the truth of things from all which seems
The sorry semblance of my aching dreams!
If thou canst lead me thither, I would reach
The pleasant havens thy mellifluous speech

Declares thine own, and on thy path attend,
However far, yea, unto the world's end.
If thou hast powers and gifts with power to give,
Let it be life, I pray, for I would live
And reach what lies beyond our mortal breath,
Wherein we eat not bread of life but death!

QUEEN

Poor youth, I pity thee; I take thy hand,
Thou hast no need to question or to fear;
I am the youngest queen in Fairyland
And but to crown thy days has brought me here!

SCHOLAR

Oh lady, listen to that voice without
My ear, so softly breathing, and such doubt
Within my soul inspiring!

QUEEN

Heed it not!
The Halls of Faerie bless the human lot,
And years as days shall pass when thou hast seen
The unveil'd beauty of an elfin queen.

SCHOLAR

Per signum Tau, per signum Tau,
Keep me, Great Lord, in Thy true law!
[*Crossing himself.*

QUEEN

Ah, woe is me! What malison
Falls on me from this gracious sign?
Ah, Light that is of all divine
And grace of grace I shall not know!
What evil has the elfin done?
My beauty and my power are mine:
Halls of Faerie, shine and shine;
Save me, save me from this woe! [*Exit* R.U.E.

SCHOLAR

Right well it doth appear that mortal life
Is all engirded with incessant strife
And bowèd with unending heaviness,
One knowledge lacking which alone can bless.
All woe is in the world, all want of love,
Because none thinketh in his heart thereof,
Nor taketh heed of the great mysteries.
Surely there lieth heal'd in all man sees
High sacrament, holy and full of grace,
Meet to transform this world's laborious place
To hill of joy, which now is vale of tears,
If we could see with eyes, and our own ears
Could open surely to the secret things.
A voice unknown continually sings
Of one who comes within the altar's pale
At the high sacring, with the Holy Graal,
And of the powerful words that there are said,
Which never enter in the learner's head,

Which no man knows, save God his soul has taught,
Though all our pain is by their absence wrought.
So speaks the voice unknown, but though I hear,
It is with clouded mind and torpid ear.
Nathless, if knowledge be our souls denied,
Full surely peace may come at altar side
And sweet humility shall bless his lot
Which kneels in worship, understanding not.
Will it not also on a tide befall
That he who follows on this poor man's call
Shall find such meaning in the mystic chant
As all good Latin scholars may not vaunt,
Since well 'tis said that he who seeks shall find
And to receive who asks good givers are inclined?
I pray Thee, therefore, fair sweet Lord of all,
That some more lowly good may me befall,
If one so worthless, even in his need,
Must for Thy lofty mercies vainly plead!
So if the great procession of the Host,
One moment granted me, should prove the most
My aspiration to demand can dare,
May I at least this vision passing fair
Keep clean within me through my days unborn,
Thus hallowing a lot perchance forlorn
With sense of the high things exceeding ken!
And, for the rest, in common ways of men
I pray at least that I may never lack
One blessing of the seeker's daily track:
In quiet hold or hermitage to find
A priest with penances my heart to shrive,

Some space of prayer to purge the wandering mind,
And those true offices which save alive
The souls of common men in every place.
Then let me pass in Thee, with so much grace
As one may have who would have trod the road
To Sarras and the spiritual abode,
If call had come, yet on a rush-strewn floor
Has been content to dwell with open door
Beneath a humble thatch,
Knowing that somewhere there is Mont Salvatch!

THE HIDDEN CHORUS

From arrow flying in the light,
  From demon wiles which lurk at noon,
From things unclean that work at night
  In stealthy mist beneath the moon,
God save and have us—waking, sleeping—
Ex hoc nunc, in His holy keeping!

The stage lightens and DOCTOR SERAPHICUS *enters,* L.U.E., *in the sorry weeds of a pilgrim, as one that is sore beset.*

DOCTOR SERAPHICUS

So, therefore, seeking still to gain our rest,
Henceforth we follow on a further quest;
No star of all the stars contains our prize—
Conceal'd in the Unearthly Paradise.

[*The* SCHOLAR *approaches with head bent and arms crossed upon his breast.*

STRANGE HOUSES OF SLEEP

Scholar

May God for ever in His keeping have
Your heart and soul! This comfortable word
In sooth is other than my ears have heard
Since first my fortune to this fastness drave;
So for the secret grace which you have brought
Suffer the gift of thanks and grateful thought!
I pray you, gentle sir, all else before,
To hold me as your servant evermore,
And if the path to Paradise, above
All nightly stars that here can manifest,
May by your grace be in clean words express'd,
I humbly say that there is set my love
And there is fix'd my only hope of rest;
Whence I would place my portion in your hands,
Obedient for such end to all commands.

Doctor Seraphicus

If that the way of paradise engage
Your mind in this green youth, it is most well,
And haply to attain it in your age
You shall not fail, good friend; but, sooth to tell,
Whatever words from lips untrain'd may fall,
Most sad distress has still a louder call,
And for this present, my great need is such,
As one that has been hurtled overmuch,
I would the rather with my failing force
Have to your charitable mood recourse.

Perchance you can me succour and anon,
When on my pilgrim journey I have gone,
God will remember, for your kindness true,
Your fair ambition and take thought on you.

SCHOLAR

Sir, I have little of the world its boon;
A scholar poor am I, who, from the rule
Full deeply laid in Aristotle's school
All recently come forth, my steps have turn'd
In quest of higher grounds than there discern'd;
And having heard that in most holy ways
High hands a cup of benediction raise
For better hallowing and healing man,
With anxious thought a certain private plan
I have sometime within my mind devised
To do my worship at that sacred shrine;
And if my worthless state be not despised
By the high comforters and dukes divine,
It is my hope the burdens of my life
To lay therein and cease henceforth from strife.
But I have tarried till the rising moon
Should shortly o'er these arches of green leaf
To quaking darkness bring her fair relief,
And in no wise from any ban exempt,
All hordes of mischief me have come to tempt.
Whence I have taken that resource which stands
Wide open to poor men in all the lands,
And being sorely like the winepress trod
Have cast my need upon the faith of God,

So here do stand and watch with empty hands.
It may be for my help that other some
Than thou, O true, sweet friend, to me shall
come;
But since thou art the first whom I have heard
To utter in this place a peaceful word,
I could not choose but think, from halls unseen
Sent for my soul's true solace thou hast been.
Yet if I err therein and thou alone
A stranger comest to a man unknown,
For aught that I can proffer in thine aid
It is thine own already, not as lent
But freely given by one sore afraid
That pauper gifts can bring to none content.

DOCTOR SERAPHICUS

These are high words, fair sir, but as you spoke
The night, which waxes late, grew passing cold;
If, 'midst your weeds, you had perchance a cloak
Wherewith I might these shrivell'd limbs enfold,
Much would I bless such gift; and you per-
chance
Would on your path to Paradise advance,
If lightly clothed, more rapidly than now.
For many saintly histories relate
What rare rewards on charity await,
So that all heaven doth this mean earth endow.
I leave my humble matter in your hands,
Not rightly knowing how your humour stands.

THE HOLY GRAAL

SCHOLAR

The night in truth is chill and much I fear
The hap of tempest, if we linger here.
Full bitterly the wind about us wails
Vague snatches of sad, antiquated tales
I well remember having heard of yore,
As sadly and more fully by the folk
In my poor village whisper'd, long before
I learn'd that there were great and wondrous things
Of which no wind or water ever sings.
It may be, sir, their immemorial loss
Doth make all Nature seem to wear a cross,
And hence she cannot comfort her dark self
Or her dejected children, but a gulf
Doth ever widen in the hearts of both.
I dare to think that could we each attain
Those certain places in a fair domain,
Where the high, holy secrets undeclared
Are treasured out of sight, then, by my troth,
One moment of their vision, if we dared
Indeed to look, would make all cold and heat
Which scourges this our temporal retreat
For ever more to us indifferent.
But till the night's keen arrows shall be spent,
Since this my wallet holds no cloak or weeds,
But some few things which spring from Plato's seeds
And one torn mass-book which I wont to use,
Do not the little I can give refuse,

And, coming close beside me, let me shield
Your age with warmth from youth which yet is
mine!
Perchance beyond the forest and the field
Some better shelter, till the sun shall shine,
A little quest may find, and I will guide
My pace by yours and any hold espied
Will search to see if it can take you in.

DOCTOR SERAPHICUS

Since every path should warily be trod,
And those the most which take at length to God;
Before this pious journey we begin,
Where loving kindness leads upon the road,
Hearing the rumours of some bless'd abode;
I would make sure, in case we part at length,
Of fit provision to sustain my strength.
Some silver coins for this is all I need:
Give them, I pray, and may your quest succeed!
I do remember, now I think, of one,
Who having such a quest as this begun,
By ghostly counsel left all goods behind;
But this would tax perchance your youthful mind.

SCHOLAR

Master, no purse have I, which, by your leave,
Has never made me sorry, since I heard
Far off the tidings of a distant word
Which could true life impart. But now I grieve

That in this matter of your need again
My anxious heart must yearn to help in vain.
Yet stay, perchance some scholar of the waste
Beyond these woods, in worldly goods well placed,
Might buy these books which I have prized full long;
Plato, like Aristotle, may be wrong;
But in this mass-book such shall find anon
The sounding grace of many an antiphon;
And I will keep them as I can in mind
Till it is granted me once more to find
A priest to shrive me from my former sins
And give me leave to serve when Mass begins. . . .
Prepared our journey in the night to take,
Pray, by your blessing, fair that journey make!

DOCTOR SERAPHICUS

Ex hoc nunc usque ad æternum sit pax vobiscum,
Et divinum auxilium maneat semper nobiscum.
Because from flowers of earth at need arise
The shining blossoms which are stars in skies,
I pray thy virgin lilies so transferr'd
May soon the chalice of thy dreams engird!
May wine of life therefrom, vouchsafed to few,
Sustain them sweetly with supernal dew!
May streams of life in thee be so reveal'd
That thou at length shalt be in life conceal'd!
Come great abstractions which at times befall
When that which once was outward and apart,
Submerged completely in the All in All,
Knows God no longer by the yearning heart,

But as the one which doth with one abide!
Taste thou the sleep which turns all worlds aside,
From age-long motions in the great abyss
To the inbreathing rest; and that is this!
Worlds beyond worlds, on thee such peace descend,
And bring the quiet night and perfect end!

SCHOLAR

I know thee now; in days I ne'er forget,
For my most high instruction, we have met
In lonely places—yea, by toiling seas,
Where thou didst give me the first mysteries.
I pray thee, being weary and oppress'd,
To take me hence into thine utter rest.

DOCTOR SERAPHICUS

A little while, herein, we come to each,
Exchanging symbols in the guise of speech;
A little while from one another go,
And at the end the greater blessings know.
Thou askest rest, and that is wisely said:
If I can give thee sleep, give thou me bread!

SCHOLAR

I do repent indeed my dearth of thought
Who no refreshment in my scrip have brought.
On other ends than food my heart was bent;
And, seeking hidden manna, felt content,

Until the great horizons are unfurl'd,
To fast through all rogations of the world. . . .

[*The* SCHOLAR *falls upon his knees in an attitude of supplication.*

Master, to whom I think that angels sing,
The poor oblation of myself I bring
And at thy feet do place for good or ill,
For thee thereon to work thy holy will.

DOCTOR SERAPHICUS

O fair, sweet Lord, with what great power dost Thou
Thy blessing to the poor of heart allow,
Who, being ask'd for things full soon made void,
Are to the uttermost unfurnish'd found,
But yet full oft have brothers overjoy'd
By treasures incorruptible, and, crown'd
In all the light of givers, the whole land
Replenish royally, with open hand,
Yet are themselves by bounty evermore
Garnish'd with precious and increasing store!
Therefore, dear scion of the elect, hereby,
Before all worlds, truly I testify
That thy free gift above vain things of earth
Is precious first by love and next by worth,
Whence I accept it from clean hands which give.
And howsoe'er blind instinct prompts to live—
In things the highest as the meanest, most
In those whose youth as yet has spent no fires—
Here comes the utmost term of thy desires
And all ambition's lightly vestured host.

Thou hast thyself surrender'd and I take
Both hermitage and hold, mine own to make,
Since verily thy life, and nothing less,
I needed when I ask'd for simple bread.
That lasts no longer than an hour's distress,
As gold, however gotten, on his head
Who taketh thought thereof, returns like lead;
As care of raiment and with cold to strive
Will hinder those who would at ends arrive,
And something seek to finish ere they move
From courts of passion to high halls of love.
Now therefore, to make end of all that means
Prolong'd dejection in these mournful scenes,
And leaves the soul unfit to travel back;
I do invite thee here to choose a track
Which, far from foolish things of birth and breath,
Will pass indeed through torrents of cold death,
But instantly thereafter wider schemes
Shall part the dream of stars from star of dreams.
Now, since the tide is late and none can tell
What follows on hereafter, let us call
Softly for help from Him which helpeth all,
And so pronounce in patience our farewell,
With *mea culpa* on the humbled breast;
The mass is over, *ite missa est.*

SCHOLAR (*having risen*)

Master, acquit it that my heart is cold
And that, as one to whom it hath been given
With foes full long and sadly to have striven,

I do thus suddenly grow worn and old !
Herein it seems as if my days had past
By many veils of darkness overcast
And now at length their pallid span expend
With bitter rendings at this ghostly end.
Yet through the shrouded gulches of the gloom,
And past your prophet voice, thus preaching doom,
Persuasive tokens of a light long miss'd
Find entrance and with late appeals persist
That in the common ways of Nature dwelt
Great joys, for ever by those hearts unfelt
Which do the cryptic paths alone applaud.
So also suddenly the frosts have thaw'd,
All turgid night from the empyrean rolls
And earthly spaces fill with happy souls.
Now, high as lark in heaven or deep as bowers
Wherein the sea heals immemorial flowers,
The world's great organ sounds through spacious
halls
And all the faithful fauna sweetly calls
To hear how priestly Nature, ere they pass,
Pontifically chants her twelvemonth mass,
And at each noon triumphantly lifts up
The Seynt Graal overbrimm'd of the sun's cup.
Meseems, immeasurable gain is loss
Perchance not less unmeasured, and the cross,
Which through the place of suffering spreads wide,
In heaven itself no less counts crucified.
But, making end of this, to die or not
For all things good in thy horizon's lot,

I do hereby, with so much of freewill
As heritors of woe reserve them still,
Make over, to accord my faithful pledge,
The life I call my own to thy sword's edge.
God grant me not with the last pang to strive
And after death's dark sting me keep alive,
That past the rubicon of this world's rim,
By paths unmanifest, I may reach Him! . . .
Let us go forth, kind sir, lest all of bliss
I, who have lost so much, at end should miss! . . .
Peccavi cogitatione, Lord—
Verbo et opere—I seek the sword!

MASTER

From substitutes of joy which pall and cease
To spiritual place, come thou in peace!
To Sarras shining in the morning land
Thee takes, by paths of peace, this guiding hand.
So shalt thou reach at length and touch the latch
Which keeps the secret door in Mont Salvatch,
And when thou tirlest trembling at the pin
The keepers of the courts shall let thee in.

SCHOLAR

I have been offer'd Wine and they which brought
Were sorry and constrain'd beyond all thought;
Then the great things went by that were not seen.
I have been offer'd Love and this has been

THE HOLY GRAAL

From everlasting the chief stay of man;
But in the heart thereof a hidden plan
Was cherish'd to delude me and undo.
Next Folly came in weeds of motley hue,
With hair unkempt, who wildly spoke anon
Of the waste years that have in wisdom gone
And counsell'd pleasant ways, the which dispense
His fond disciples from all sober sense.
But I had learn'd some elements in books
Whereat the Masters cast disdainful looks,
And thus, although imperfectly equipp'd,
Our bales to ports asunder straight were shipp'd.
In fine, it fell that being left alone,
With less than little I could call my own,
There gleam'd, with clouded grace and helping hand,
A queen emerging out of Faerie Land
Who, past the woful gate of human tears,
Did offer anodynes for misspent years.
Then in my heart such strong desire was bred
That spells to save from self seem'd needed then
For me so strongly tried by maids and men.
But at one orison that fair dame fled,
For whom I pray no less the cross may come
At length in healing, as to other some.
So in great dark once more alone I dwelt,
Until the magic of thy voice was felt
Conversing, as from other years than these,
Of life for life and such deep mysteries.
And though it sounds to me a mournful word,
Thus on the early verge of manhood heard,

STRANGE HOUSES OF SLEEP

I do believe, dear master, being thine,
That it is medicine more than anodyne.
But ere my sacrifice completed strips
My one possession, let thy patient lips
Declare, I pray thee, since they are so wise—
Beyond most wit—in these high mysteries:
What is that secret lore which may expound
Wherefore man is so sorry on this round
Of earthly things, why nought of joyance is
Which at the end falls not to him amiss?

DOCTOR SERAPHICUS

Surely the answer doth most plain appear—
It is the secret of man being here.

SCHOLAR

What then, amidst his stress and its sharp pain,
Shall be the greatest thing that he can gain?

DOCTOR SERAPHICUS

Who runs shall read herein: great gain they find
Who to be here no more apply their mind.

SCHOLAR

But how and whither shall the mind be bent
Which being here no more, is then content?

THE HOLY GRAAL

DOCTOR SERAPHICUS

Thus it is with him who, by God his grace,
Gains that which makes all ways the Holy Place.

SCHOLAR

How shall the greatest treasure under heaven
To man of poor desert be truly given?

DOCTOR SERAPHICUS

If, having sought in vain through things without,
To find its gate within he turns about.

SCHOLAR

I pray thee, take me on to thy far goal!
My flesh is weary of itself and drags
A chain which sorely past all longing lags.
Receive my life and let me see my soul!
Too long have we been parted in the ways
Which lead so far from any peace or praise.

[DOCTOR SERAPHICUS *takes the* SCHOLAR *by the arm and leads him up stage, as if moving eastward.*

DOCTOR SERAPHICUS

Line upon line, and there is none left out
When earthly shades in fine are put to rout.

SCHOLAR

In manus tuas; fair, sweet Lord of all;
Thy Thorns shall crown me and Thy Cross enthrall!

DOCTOR SERAPHICUS

Thus through the night, as through the wells most cold
Which must the passing soul receive and fold,
I take thee by a path which from the West
Leads forth—*mysterium consummatum est*—
The mystery of mortal life—and thus
In depths beyond all deeps of perfect peace
Perchance the East on high shall visit us,
Who in such light expect the heart's increase.

[*Solemn music is heard and a great light kindles behind the curtains. Two young men in white and gold draperies of the Second Order of the Graal come forward and clothe the* SCHOLAR *in the marriage robe of the Sanctuary. This is done in silence and the young men return* E., *parting the curtains of the Sanctuary, so that the Shrine within is exposed for the second time, with the* BISHOP *and the Priests of the Graal, the Stewards and the Acolytes grouped as for the close of Mass. The* BISHOP *puts down the Cup as the curtains open. Thereat* DOCTOR SERAPHICUS *takes the* SCHOLAR *towards the curtain, saying:*

THE HOLY GRAAL

Doctor Seraphicus

Domine, non sum dignus ut intres sub tectum meum, sed tantum dic verbo et sanabitur anima mea.

[*The* Scholar *kneels at the Shrine.*

The Hidden Chorus *of Clean Offerings breathes out very softly and solemnly behind the Holy Place of the Shrine.*

Chorus

From day to day, because of human sins,
O'er all the world the blessed Mass begins.

From day to day, ere that oblation ends,
A certain far-off peace on earth descends.

The secret centre offers mutely up
The inward mystery of the outward cup.

That which on earth is validly begun
In many places, here conjoins in one.

Thereby, in the good pleasure of the Lord,
All toiling worlds shall be to rest restored.

Doctor Seraphicus

Seeing, high brethren and adepts exempt,
That outward vestures for a time may tempt
The children of desire; but in the end
Their tribulation's strong appeals ascend

And mercy cometh from the mercy seat;
I, even I, the Steward of the Graal,
Was with full powers commission'd to estreat
Some certain wiles encompassing the feet
Of this our son and brother, lest he fail.
Now, having the allotted tests applied,
With those purgations to his need allied,
I bring him hither, by your holy leave,
Some token of your favour to receive,
That his translation may, by saving grace,
From seeming death to very life take place.

The HIDDEN CHORUS *of Clean Offerings chants solemnly behind the Holy Place of the Shrine.*

CHORUS

Once on the threshold of this life's distress
The steward of the mysteries, to keep
Intact a certain narrow space of sleep,
Proffer'd the chalice of forgetfulness.
Then man's departing soul, amidst its fears,
Stoop'd and thereof drank deep,
Forecasting toil of unfelicitous years
And the long aching past the gate of tears.
Hence it befalls that in the show which seems
There is but dreaming and the dreamer's schemes,
And no true waking can to man befall
Whose hold has loosed upon the life of all

And the great treasures which do perish not.
It doth behove us therefore, sadly placed
Like this, if it may be, to mend our lot
And seek one high light shining in the waste
Whose beacon, lifted through the dark, can bring
Alone our soul to its awakening.
So past the gate of tears at length it sees
That chasten'd steward of the mysteries
Lift, on the threshold of the things which be,
A consecrated cup of memory.

[*The* BISHOP *of the* GRAAL *turns with extended arms pronouncing the* Dominus Vobiscum. *At the raising of the Cup, the* SCHOLAR *falls upon his face; the Deacons gather about him in a semicircle. The* HIDDEN CHORUS *of Clean Offerings again breathes out, but this time triumphantly.*

CHORUS

Hac die laetus meruit beatas
Scandere sedes.

FINIS

PART III

THE POOR BROTHER'S MASS-BOOK

When so much fails the soul; when lights in flashes
   First coruscate, then die; the paths we trod
And the green life about them burnt to ashes—
   What then remains? The soul's return to God.
Beyond the Orders and the Churches rise
The great and secret heights. The soul descries,
Through an immeasurable distance, how
Ascent is possible in fine for all
Who do no proffer'd graces disavow.
And seeing that the nearest door perchance
Is that intended for her first advance,
Less as a home at first than house of call
She to the Church appeals for ministries.
Haply it follows that the soul, who there
Enters on inward offices of prayer—
Despite the letter and its grievous chain—
Shall find the Church has all and there remain.

THE POOR BROTHER'S MASS-BOOK

THE POOR BROTHER'S MASS-BOOK

OR A DEVOUT METHOD OF ASSISTING AT THE HOLY SACRIFICE FOR CHILDREN WHO ARE NOT OF THIS WORLD. ITEM: AN IMPLIED MANNER OF SERVING, FOR CLERKS OF THE HOLY ASSEMBLIES.

I
WHEN PASSING THE THRESHOLD OF THE TEMPLE

The postulant enters the outward Church, to partake of its ministry, as one who accepts for the moment the second best, while desiring those things which are supernal.

GREATER DISILLUSION

BEHOLD we stand from all deceit apart!
Nothing misleads us, nothing can betray;
We have reckon'd up all vanities and seek
True life alone, asking for God through all,
Having outgrown his sacraments and types

And yet deferring to their ministry,
As to the service of green leaves at noon
And all the votive offerings Nature brings—
Odours of sweetness, myrrh, frankincense, gold.

While men are seeking for truth with many clamours, God opens the door of the heart and comes in.

II

WHEN TAKING SEAT

The Postulant assumes his appointed place with perfect conformity, under obedience to the instituted signs, invoking the Voice and the Word.

The Voice of the Beloved

That which we heard of old, and long to hear,
Speak in the floods once more, or, far and near,
Amidst the rushing winds reverberate;
In the sea's music, mother of thought profound
And deepest feeling, let the tidings sound;
Most in thought's silent ways, early and late!

The Second Temple was not less the House of God because the Shekinah was withdrawn.

THE POOR BROTHER'S MASS-BOOK

III

THE FIRST RECOLLECTION

The soul exhorts herself, because paths of advance in the several grades of the Lesser and Greater Mysteries are in a certain sense narrow, and few enter the Gate which leads to the Higher Palace.

Le Moyen de Parvenir

STRAIGHT as the path which leads at some far
point
To the large issues of the narrow gate,
Be our life shaped in all its ways and aims,
And let all high intent the heart anoint;
But do not bide till we can meet all claims,
Or, with the chance of service, stand and wait!

It is with the great matters of religion as it is with the business of life; if we looked for time and opportunity, we should do but little in the latter, and if we tarried in the other to increase worthiness, we should never go back to God. It might be written that we shall be worthy when we enter into the Divine Union.

STRANGE HOUSES OF SLEEP

IV

A PREFATORY MEDITATION

The sun rises in the East to restore the blessing of daylight, and another sun, rising in the soul of man, brings peace as well as justice.

And so Onward

Through all earth's days the spirit and the flesh
Maintain their strife within; but our life's star
Illumines still the intellectual air,
Strength, beauty, brilliance gathering as it mounts,
Till slowly upward soars man's nobler self
Towards calmer zones, to zeniths of the mind
Aspiring. Necessary helps vouchsafed
Our weakness strengthen—most, O mighty sea,
Thy vastness and thy voices, strength with strength
Enduing! And ye too, ye lonely roads,
Ye thickets only by the fox and bird
Frequented, and ye populous human haunts—
One whole gigantic heart, throbbing with life—
Ye also help in your own high degree!
But when these fail us, as our last resource,
The House of God remains to take us in;
And if to hearts inhibited at times

The ministrations in the Holy Place
Seem voided, know, the Master of the House,
With signs of presence, shall at need invest
Both inward chancel and external nave!

We cannot suppose that the man is approaching God who has obviously no desire thereof; but we must hope that deep in his heart there may still be a latent capacity of that desire.

V

THE CEREMONY OF COMMENCING THE OFFICE

The Great Mysteries of Religion, as represented by their Liturgical Rites, begin invariably with invocation of the Divine Names by the way of that substitution which signifies, in a summary, the whole mission of the Church, being the reverent and orderly communication of great auguries and tokens which stand for things not manifest: *e.g.* the *In Nomine* which opens the Mass.

The Secret Name

The letters of the Name we long to learn
Are found in sacred books at every turn,
Yet we in vain those characters may trace
Which simple scholars in the class discern;
For the Great Name itself, our saving grace,
Is utter'd only in the Holy Place.

The atmosphere of the Divine Secret consists in a great disinterest.

VI

INTROIBO AD ALTARE DEI

It is good to enter the Path which takes the Seeker to the Altar, for Heaven comes down to the soul which cannot ascend thereto.

The Other Way

We tried all paths, nor found a road in one;
Sought many things beneath the wintry sun
  Which shines alone on this dim earth of ours;
But when the barren strife at length was done
  Grace came free-handed, with unlook'd for dowers,
  And shew'd the true way strewn with deathless flowers.

The youth of the soul is the King's Presence and the joy which cometh thereof is morning's joy and the Mass-time.

THE POOR BROTHER'S MASS-BOOK

VII

JUDICA ME, DEUS

He who prays to be delivered from the evil man asks to be saved from himself.

THE CAUSE PLEADED

WE have confess'd Thee since our days began,
Thy providence discern'd in every man,
And yet unprofitable servants still
Remain, so distant from Thy holy hill;
Conscious of nothing like the dreadful want
  And void within us full of rumours dark,
Waiting Thy manifested covenant,
  The refuge of Thine Altar and Thine Ark.

The soul is sad and disturbed because of the great distance; but this is a part of her illusion.

VIII

THE CONFESSION

The *Sanctum Sanctorum* is the place of purification, and wretched is he who waits to put off his sins before he has recourse to God.

Foundations of Victory

A little while in the ways unknown—
   One little life—have I sought—
Or possibly many lives—to find
That truth of truth which can fill the mind;
Nor have I fear'd to stand alone
   In the lonely ways of thought.

The false lights came and the false lights went;
   I did not tarry for these;
The dreadful sense of a heart unfit,
Through its native earth—how I fought with it
And the knowledge of days mis-spent
   In face of the destinies!

If once, but once, I have sunk and said:
"Yield, Soul!" or, "The Dream is done,
Because alone the untainted heart
Wins crowns I work for!" Then, Hope, depart!
But 'twas up with the stricken head,
Still looking to meet the sun.

Therefore I hope that a soul on fire
For weal has the wine-press trod,
And though my sins upon either hand,
In witness rising, against me stand,
They shall waste not my heart's desire,
Which out of them leaps to God.

As time goes on, we desire more and more the white walls of Salem; but it should be remembered that the Eternal City is within.

IX

THE INDULGENCE

There are the greater benedictions, but, like these, the greater evils are within, and though forgiveness can be always presupposed in virtue of that supernatural love which casts out fear, there is still the mal-ease of the soul in the peopled darkness and the purlieus where the commerce of wickedness drives its several trades.

Presages

On common auguries and omens, long
Has man in legend dwelt, in tale and song,
   And under thin disguise they hold him still;
But to the body and its varied need
His signs and auguries alone give heed,
Leaving those deeper symbols all unread
Which say: The soul is sick, the soul is dead,
   The soul is menaced by surpassing ill.
Fear not malignant stars which may control
The outward fortunes; fear those stars within
Which on the wide horizon of the soul
   With baleful rays illume the night of sin!

It is in the suspension of earthly things that the first secret consists.

X

WHEN THE PRIEST ASCENDS TO THE ALTAR

The search after God is not the quest of joy, which itself is the counsel of the search, but the satisfaction of a craving impelled by the spur of necessity.

THE LAST END

WHEN after all the strife and wearying
We come in contact with the great true thing,
  Which points the term of all—will that be such
  As will make compensation overmuch
For the long disillusions and sharp sting?
  Who knows? This only—its most distant touch
Thrills our heart's instrument in every string.

It is not impossible to aspire to the similitude of God.

XI

AUFER A NOBIS

Man is a time-piece which never stops.

Purgation

A LITTLE space of daylight and of gloom,
Of pain and dim delight, and then the tomb,
   Whereat the whole is over and is gone;
Those scenes forget us where of old we toil'd—
Sad is it surely, but the soul assoil'd
   Its path appointed takes, and still goes on.
Now, therefore, where Thy Holy Place begins,
Bid us, we pray Thee, pause, and purge our sins!

Let us seek to enter with pure minds, but remember that enter we must.

XII

THE INTROIT

It is the concealment of God in humanity which causes the sleep of this life.

An Opening of the Gates

According to our measure and extent,
Despite long exile in these regions dim,
We must from God compute our soul's descent,
Seeing the soul on Him alone is bent,
And must in that degree partake of Him.

Believe in the great things, practise mansuetude and sweetness!

XIII

THE KYRIE ELEISON

We do not enter the Path because it is pleasant, but because it is the only path.

The Gate and the Way

A narrow gate, a straight, unbending road,
Bleak hill-tops, sudden gorges, and a load
Of sadness through the solitary track:
One comfort only—to our own abode
The one way back!
And since we needs must reach Thee, why and how
Esteeming little, shew us mercy, Thou!

It is not becoming that those who were born in the palace should build cabins in the desert.

XIV

GLORIA IN EXCELSIS

The places of peace are also those of exaltation.

The Secret of Success

Peace in high places; on the peaks supreme,
Far over passion's mists, deep peace of love;
Light of true light, the glory and the gleam;
Far over troubled sleep, what worlds of dream
Give space for souls—yes, there is room above!

Sleep naturally passes into dream, but there is a certain repose in which dream is exalted into vision; and this at its induction is initiation, but at the end, adeptship.

XV

THE COLLECT

The consolation which carries us along is that, seeing there is but one true road no one can err therein.

Consummation

Fear not frustration of our good intent,
 But fear the feeble working of our wills;
Fail'd never yet the soul which seeking went,
Far as soul could, upon the great ascent:
What by the Word Divine—say, God—is meant?
 He that fulfils!

Do not despise the trifles, but do not let them deceive us!

XVI

THE SUBSTITUTED EPISTLE

The way of compassion is also the way of sorrow.

Ascetic Life

THE end of self-denial
  Is not to rack the flesh,
Of needless pain to heart and brain
  Adding a burden fresh.

It is to school the spirit
  And that shall teach the sense
How patience meek through all must seek,
  And yet through all dispense;

Must look for love the perfect,
  For truth the perfect end;
Not for the prize before the eyes
  But that unseen contend.

Yet must it strive, provided
  To fail on earth of each;
Must nurse no doubt but still hold out
  To reach what's out of reach.

STRANGE HOUSES OF SLEEP

The lesser purpose round it
  Shall gain the lesser meed,
And take its fill; the greater, still
  Go empty and in need.

The world unfolds her treasures;
  It sighs but does not stay;
O'er secret parts of human hearts
  It yearns, but moves away.

Perchance its goal awaits it:
  We dream but do not see;
If we but knew, our pains were few—
  Ah, light our task would be!

Task, do I say? What spirit
  Would pause on things of earth,
Did bright and clear that star appear
  Whence all our stars draw birth?

To act as if with knowledge
  Is here meanwhile our lot,
And to forego but not to know,
  Asking, but answer'd not.

One thing is certain only—
  That which we burn to find
Earth cannot give; for this to live
  Dares not the man of mind.

And so by self-denial
His greater schools his less,
'Twixt soul and star to lift no bar—
Because the end may bless.

O well for those who labour
Their daily bread to eat,
And God at last bless those who fast,
Desiring ghostly meat!

The Path of the Cross is the Path of the Mystical Rose, though Rose and Cross are joined. That which they form together is also a path of sorrow.

XVII

THE GRADUAL

Great are the heights and great also are the deeps; the cohorts of witnesses are numberless; but beyond all is the place of benediction, and to this we look for the power and the glory also.

Benison

Thou who dost bless us, whom we bless, hereby,
Before all men, I rise and testify
That by Thy grace alone I look to live;

That Thy dear gifts above the crowns of earth
Are precious, being mine by right of birth,
And hence I freely take, as Thou dost give.

There is a certain confusion of thought concerning the Divine complacency in the dedication of our human love. Even in the spheres that we seek for, it is not entirely a question of complacency, but of the natural conjunction of things which from the beginning were meant for one another.

XVIII

MUNDA COR MEUM

Though it is impossible to recall the past, the future can at least be moulded newly in respect of our plans concerning it.

The Enkindling Stone

Come, let us pledge the heart to purer life,
Thrusting the past behind, with all it holds
Of fair and dark! Come, take with stalwart front
The future! Thither—to the mountain heights!—
We yet shall meet the messenger divine,
Standing serene in some uplifted place
On which the stars shed influence, whereon
Do moon and sun concur. His hands shall hold
The shining stone inscribed with secret words
Which hallow lips for prophecy, and give,
Not only tidings true but sense thereof.

Man is native to the heights, and the burden of his normal life is a difficulty of respiration in the deeps to which he does not belong by his origin.

THE POOR BROTHER'S MASS-BOOK

XIX

THE FIRST GOSPEL

It is therefore only on the mountains that the feet of the messenger are beautiful when he brings glad tidings near.

ON THE WAY TO JERUSALEM

UNHALLOW'D exhalations, steaming up
From passion's burning sacrifice, becloud
The altar height whereon the soul enthroned
Sits, like a sibyl on the divining seat,
And raves, inebriate with the ascending fumes.
Who looks abroad, commanding life and time?
Who calm in conscious strength her crown awaits?
Child of the Greater Dawn, not thou, long call'd
But chosen not; in madness revelling! . . .
O if the splendours of the life above
This turbid life of earth might dawn on us,
With shafts of sacred light and two-edged beams
Refracted up and down from rocks and peaks
Of spiritual precipice, to rend
This temple's veil, this temple built by flesh
To flesh for the soul's bondage and dark night;
And the soul freed, among the dateless hills
Some path discern, that follow'd evermore
Might lead to Zion, the eternal town,
The endless rest! Receive thine exiled child,

High city, set upon the hills; from far,
How far, across life's turbid, unanneal'd
And questing waters, from the murk and waste,
Where upas vapours breathe, we hail thee now,
Suspiring towards thee! And thy gospel bells
Proclaim new hopes when souls redeem'd by Thee
Shall gaze abroad, commanding life and time,
And calm in conscious strength the crown await.

Salem is on the mountain top because it is a spiritual city.

XX

THE CREDO

Those truths which most call for expression are those also which exceed it.

Inexpressible

Now, let us here in secret, as if drawn
  Together in some holy place apart
To welcome in the day-star ere it dawn,
  Declare the hidden matter—heart to heart:
Nay, it eludes the thought, however high,
And words still fail him who would testify.

The fact that there is one issue for everything and one test by which alone it can be judged does not interfere with the other fact that there is more than one answer to most questions, or that the gifts of interpretation are various. We continue, therefore, to say: *Credo in unum Deum.*

XXI

THE OFFERTORY

It is a little thing to renounce extrinsic goods, having already renounced ourselves.

True Possessions

Much does he gain who much dispenses; want
Shall reach him not, a constant stream of wealth
Is round him drawn. From him who meanly
 hoards
His own, is true wealth taken. What in one
Centres alone is lost, and every gift—
Not in the man inherent—whether sent
From God directly or from Nature, shared,
Returns to the dispenser; we attain
All things in giving and renouncing them.

With the things which are of real value we have never been asked to part, but only with those tokens which are of temporal convenience, some of which become encumbrances and even burdens.

XXII

THE OBLATION

There is a reason why silence envelopes us within in spite of the clamours that are without; yet the expression of the higher soul is the only clean offering, and this is imposed upon us.

Expression

All that once we meant to say
  Deep within the heart of each
Rests unutter'd. Tell me, pray,
  When shall man have leave for speech?

Ah, the long unspoken soul,
  Thus with message overcharged,
Underneath its bonds' control
  Is, in spite of bonds, enlarged!

Deeper sinks the depth within,
  All horizons melt from sight,
Till life's mighty waters win
  Union with the infinite.

Deep to deep and sea to sea,
  Wondrous union, wondrous rest,
And o'erflowing, then shall be
  The long pent-up soul express'd.

The need of expression arises from the law of concealment, but this law is essential and inheres rather than is imposed. For the same reason the burden of sin is imposed, but the yoke of grace is native and so also is light.

XXIII

THE MINGLING OF WINE AND WATER

From the centre to the circumference may be far, but the way is direct to the end. The union of elements is in motion and therefore man goes on.

The Higher Circumstance

Perchance from distant haven, further star,
And thence beyond where any systems are,
Cometh a man's soul on this earthly ground,
With whose high offices the ways resound
A little while, till he is taken far,
Leaving the rumours of his body and mind
To echo long before him and behind.
Meanwhile from other star or shining sun
Comes here a second to replace that one;

But having gather'd up his own he goes
And unescorted must in turn ascend:
So from its source unseen the pageant flows,
For ever passing to the unseen end.

Watchman, what of the end?

XXIV

IN SPIRITU HUMILITATIS

The power of arbitration in man is between the heights and the deeps, but the place of peace is not in the middle way.

Two Destinies

Some men no doubt class best with Nature's mimes—
Theirs is the lighter task. No sports of Fate
Are we—such wise ones! Of his doom is each
The arbiter; it lies between his hands,
A plastic clay, either to shape or mar.
Recall that antique fable of the Keys
Some statue's hand uplifted in the waste:
Each had fatality attached thereto;
Who shot for them inherited! We all
Aim thus to find our dooms and so become
Of our own fate the agents. We are free
To choose a course, but, chosen, each must bear
Its true, inevitable consequence.
The keys of wealth, calamity and pain,

Of power, of death, of immortality,
And every dole attaching unto these,
We hold; as victors o'er adversity,
Conquerors of love and hate, the masters still,
Can, if we choose, emerge, nor e'er be bound;
Nor into misery and abjectness
Need ever fall, but great through all may be,
Forth issuing exultant in the end.
Count therefore this the spirit and the term
Of our condign humility, which knows
That being what we were, we yet must be
More than a laurell'd Cæsar triumphing,
Though sold as bondsmen in the market-place
Which makes our exile in these alien ways!

It is not a matter of importance that the victory should be ultimately with ourselves, but the great ends must prevail, and they can prevail only in us.

XXV

IN THE BLESSING OF BREAD AND WINE

It is possible to receive God in many elements.

Venite

Weary of walking in the night alone,
Come, we beseech Thee, come unto Thine own!
Vapid are our pursuits and vain our lot
But not so foolish we as to receive Thee not.

Communication is in many kinds but the true act of reception is only in the inmost heart.

XXVI

THE INCENSING OF THE BREAD AND WINE

The soul is naturally fastidious, and even the manna in the wilderness calls for express consecration.

Probation

Of many elements combined, we plead
For Thy great blessing to assuage our need
In this wide world of dreams!
God grant that, issuing at last from these,
We shall unlock, with certain secret keys,
Life's inmost and far curving galleries,
Where very singers find the very themes!

The opening of the closed palace is a great work of inspiration.

XXVII

THE INCENSING OF THE ALTAR

Seasons of inhibition are promises of seasons of fulness.

Interdiction

THE time of blessing comes and goes;
  Then dry days follow for a space,
That learners may their hearts dispose
  To walk at need apart from grace.
Say therefore not that grace is dead,
  Say not that aspiration's fount,
Henceforth to flow inhibited,
  Is seal'd up in the sacred mount!
Say rather: muteness full and rich
  In its still depths prepares the ground
For other wells of mercy, which
  In later torrents shall abound!

The soundings of the deep are beyond the plummets of the senses.

XXVIII

ACCENDAT IN NOBIS

It does not signify whether joy comes in the morning, but it is vital that the King should come.

The Unities

Diverse our passions, yet but one desire;
Much smoke, much smouldering, one cleansing
  fire;
Concerns unnumber'd which are little blest,
    Only one rest,
One travail that is worthy of the hire—
The labour, the heart's burning and the dumb,
Unspoken longing for the King to come
And his great kingdom to be manifest!

Most of us perhaps can do little to assist its manifestations in the world, but we can cherish it secretly in the heart.

XXIX

BEFORE THE LAVABO

It is well to wash with the innocent, but it is a greater thing to go through the cleansing fires which purge the guilty from their sins.

Misfits

'Tis scarcely true that souls come naked down
To take abode up in this earthly town,
   Or naked pass, of all they wear denied;
We enter slipshod and with clothes awry,
And we take with us much that by-and-bye
   May prove no easy task to put aside.

Cleanse therefore that which round about us
      clings,
   We pray Thee, Master; ere thy sacred halls
We enter, strip from us redundant things
   And meetly clothe us in pontificals!

The House of God is the House of many Lustrations.

XXX

SUSCIPE, SANCTA TRINITAS

The first consummations are only the first draughts of the everlasting cup; but the secret is to drink deeply.

Journeys in the Blue Distance

A little space to move in, and a little space for sleep,
And then a space more narrow for repose that is more deep;
Then all the vistas open'd, and the strange high paths untrod,
With room for men to walk in who go forth to find their God.
We offer up ourselves and Thine are made;
All other bonds our wills at least evade:
But do Thou give us of Thyself and thus
A clean oblation shall be made by us!
Thou dost not need our offerings, but we
Transmuting need, to make us gold for Thee.

The greatest quests are not those which are followed in time or space.

THE POOR BROTHER'S MASS-BOOK

XXXI

SECRETA

So long as we are exiled from God, we can scarcely escape sin.

Restoration

I came into the world for love of Thee,
  I left Thee at Thy bidding;
I put off my white robes and shining crown
And came into this world for love of Thee.

I have lived in the grey light for love of Thee,
  In mean and darken'd houses:
The scarlet fruits of knowledge and of sin
Have stain'd me with their juice for love of Thee.

I could not choose but sin for love of Thee,
  From Thee so sadly parted;
I could not choose but put away my sin
And purge and scourge those stains for love of Thee.

My soul is sick with life for love of Thee,
  Nothing can ease or fill me:
Restore me, past the frozen baths of death,
My crown and robes, desired for love of Thee:

And take me to thyself for love of Thee;
  My loss or gain counts little,
But Thou must need me since I need Thee so,
Crying through day and night for love of Thee!

The wings of the dove would not carry us into rest, for a bird's flight bears the same relation to progress that a sand castle bears to Mont Salvatch in the Pyrenees.

XXXII

SURSUM CORDA

The exaltation of the heart takes place after many purgations.

Secret Song

O sad voice singing close at hand,
Thy words we may not understand!
But strangely full and sweet art thou;
And thou dost soothe, we know not how.
Perchance thy low refrain reveals,
In sorrow's deeps, the well which heals.

A great pity must surge for ever in the soul of the illuminated man towards all motions and yearnings of Nature, so full of impassioned endeavour, so full of the sense of loss and inability.

THE POOR BROTHER'S MASS-BOOK

XXXIII

THE PREFACE

It is a long watch to the morning, but it is also a sure one.

The Day After

Sufficient to the night was sleep, and late
We enter slowly on the waking state,
  Uncertain yet if all the dreams be past;
But having drunk of poppies we collect,
A little band, to watch, with heads erect,
  If anyhow the day should break at last.

The powers and the glories are with us in the great vigil, and the darkness of the night intervening is no ground for doubt in the heart.

XXXIV

THE CANON

All the greater laws are made in the course of our advancement.

Facilis Ascensus

What is the canon of the King's true law,
  By which we know it is indeed the King's?
Ah, could we find it—faithful, free from flaw—
Clear would be all which once we dimly saw
  And simple the ascent to noble things!

The official interpretations of laws are like sonorous but confused voices of great winds surging about a secret sanctuary.

XXXV

COMMEMORATION OF THE LIVING

There is a great past behind us and the future as great is in front.

Nunc Dimittis

How perfect is the peace of him
  Whose work in life is done,
And space remains to count the gains
  Of some high course outrun;

Who looking back on his past track
  Can proudly lift the head
And truly claim for every aim—
  This is consummated.

In spite of our dreaming and our seeming, we have begun to touch the reality in this life, because the sacramental body of man is the sum of all physical perfection which it is possible for us here to conceive.

XXXVI

THE CONSECRATION AND ELEVATION

The man who denies the sacraments is less guilty than he who dismembers them.

Of Bread and Wine

From the first dawn of things Thou hast me fed
With many substances of wine and bread
Beyond those daily charities which bless
All men with manna in the wilderness;
Yea, in that time when I was lifted up
Refreshment from an everlasting cup
To take with spiritual lips, Thou didst
My soul sustain, its angel-peers amidst.
Then at Thy board I sat, all sane and whole,
Clothed in the proper garment of my soul;

And in the liturgies and rites which make
A rapture in Thy presence, I did take
A part allotted, and their calls fulfil
With a most clear remembrance of Thy will.

But after, for some purpose undeclared,
From Thy great temple's service I was spared;
From Thy high palace-gates and halls sent down
And precincts fair of Thine eternal town—
I know not why, who had not tired of Thee
And scarce could falter in Thy ministry,
Under Thine eyes' light, with such graces lent—
Sufficing, efficacious. But I went,
And since that time, which is earth's time outside,
Far as my paths might from Thy throne divide,
Deep as the depths might be which I plunged in—
Conduits and cesspools of the House of Sin—
In the strange tavern and the stranger's bed,
I do remember still Thy wine and bread.

Thus having pass'd into this low estate,
So that I cannot look up to Thy gate;
Having withal too dim and sad an eye
To see the splendour of that chancelry,
Where, unto those who serve and those who err,
Justice or love Thou dost administer;
I have been long content Thy hands to bless
For any manna in the wilderness:
But, though all gifts within Thy hands are good,
My soul now turns and loathes this lighter food;

Such froth upon the surface cannot feed
The man whose want demands strong meat and
mead.
Therefore as one who has been raised from base
And scullion errands to a page's place,
My need has bade me from the broken meat
And brings me, crying, at Thy board to eat;
And, since all bridal garments here I lack,
I call on Thee to give those vestments back
Wherein I served in such uplifted state
Ere I was put forth from Thy palace gate:
Still through all straits I kept my claim on
them
And the bright shining of my diadem.

Perchance I fell from Thee through mine own
fault;
Yet am I native to Thy temple vault;
Perhaps, for Thine own purpose, Thou hast seen
Fit to reduce me from my primal mien;
But be my guilt in Thine eyes less or more
Now matters not: I pray—Restore, restore!
And having given, as Thou needs must give,
To one who naked can no longer live,
The proper garments of the soul, I know
That to Thy banquet hall I then shall go,
Saying: "High Master, I have fasted long;
Give me man's meat and wine of vintage strong."
Whereat, with fitting benison and grace,
They shall set down true bread before my place

And to my lips Thy pages shall lift up—
For deep, free drinking—an eternal cup.

Therefore, by all who hear these high words said
In the King's sense be they interpreted.

We can always be sure of our commentaries, short as they fall of perfection, by uniting their intention with God.

XXXVII

THE COMMEMORATION OF THE DEAD

The life of earth is an experience of things unfamiliar: the after life is a renewal of the old familiarity.

Restoration

As by his own fireside, in his own chair,
A man slips gently into sleep, and there
Starts up awake once more in his own room,
Recalling all things in the glow and gloom;
So when the draught of death in sleep he takes,
Perchance all suddenly the man awakes
To find him in the old familiar place,
That primal home, left for life's little space.

That which is not known is that which we have forgotten.

IBID

We are so much on the verge of the union that it seems almost impossible we should escape it.

Ghost's Hollow

Over the bridge and athwart the stream—
In a land that I call my own—
Is another land that I visit in dream,
And dreamers term it the world unknown.
The paths are clouded, the hollows are dim,
And a pallid and misty host
Is moving there with a vacant air,
For this is the Land of Ghost.

As a Land of Ghost is the Land of Soul;
O Wraiths of the viewless bourne!
Do you hear, as I hear, the waters roll
In the rain of the tears of those who mourn?
The darkness deepens, the darkness spreads:
We shrink from the downward track
Which far through the hollow takes those who follow,
For who that descends comes back?

But there falls a night or a day will dawn
When a hand unseen lays hold,
And into the hollow we slip, withdrawn
Over the grey lawns shrouded and cold.

STRANGE HOUSES OF SLEEP

Over the brook by the bridge we go,
  Sorrowing voices still'd behind;
But dole or laughter, who knows what after,
  Or what of the end assign'd?

Who knows? Who knows? From the further side
  Perchance on a spectral host,
Far over a resonant, splendid tide,
  Back we shall gaze on a Land of Ghost
(For a Land of Ghost is this land of life,
  With its phantom joys and woes):
From a great true dream upon pomps which seem—
  We shall gaze at that last—who knows?

We have been cautious through many initiations, but a great reservation must be taken into the grade *ne plus ultra* of death.

IBID

Those who have gone before us are so much the nearer to the Union.

MANIFESTATION

A FIGURE sat within the chair
Which was not previously there;
A voice spoke in the darkness then
More subtly than the voice of men;
The message in the ear it spell'd—
Was one great secret long withheld;
And while I live, or when I die,
O grave! where is thy mystery?

The secrets are not spoken but signified.

IBID

We look at the end of things for Hades to return its spoils.

Dies Venit

Now heralds, passing through desponding Hades,
Proclaim : "*Salvete !* O my Lords and Ladies,
Here ends the penance, here unbars the prison ;
Into the light ascend, for He is risen !"

The Hades into which Christ descended corresponds to the visible world, which keeps many spirits in prison besides those that are ostensibly sharing our exile. The Mystery of the Passion and of that Lamb which has been slain from the foundation of the world is one of the mysteries of the unseen. The true Golgotha and Calvary are not of this world.

XXXVIII

NOBIS QUOQUE PECCATORIBUS

The greatest work in the world is that of building bridges.

De Profundis

Though oft I have fallen by the way, Mother mine,
Yet I have not turn'd my face aside from thee ;
And Father, loving Father, in the world that is thine
Thy great white light of glory I have look'd to see.

Take me then, for I am weary, I beseech thee,
  And I do not dread the gulfs or wastes between!
Lift me upward, being merciful, to reach thee,
  If I cannot cross the seas that intervene!

But even the intervening seas are the emanations of mercy.

XXXIX

PATER NOSTER

The invocation of the Kingdom is also the invocation of ravishment.

The Kingdom

From place to place, with all its gardens girt,
Slow moves the mystic city of mirage,
Turret and spire and dome and belfry high,
While all who look thereon do evermore
Carry strange longings in their haunted eyes.
Oh fanes and palaces for chosen souls!
Oh floral emblems! oh prophetic trees!
Oh visionary voices—the long days
And nights enchanting—of thy streams, thy birds!
Oh, dream of things which vanish at a touch!—
What lights shall lead us into those which last?—
Oh purple splendours, infinite ecstasy!

The food of the visible frame is also the body of God.

XL

LIBERA NOS, QUÆSUMUS

When man enters into the Holy Place, the Kingdom comes.

Fellowship

When darkness falls upon the life of mind;
When utter sickness to the heart assign'd
  Makes morbid thoughts on all our days intrude;
When uncompanion'd in our need we stand,
One is still with us in the shrouded land—
  Our own soul with us in the solitude.
Set therefore free the soul and let her cease
  From evil, knowing what is right and wrong;
  And seeing that her days in Thine are long
Grant that her endless days be also peace!

He who has found his soul is never alone.

XLI

AGNUS DEI

Both the emissary and the imputation are in one sense the symbolical embroideries of pontifical vestments.

The Better Way

Our hearts, disdainful in these days, repent
That poor ambition and unwise content,
Which, in the midst of veil and semblance, left—
Of the sole true realities bereft—
Those high prerogatives of human mind
Call'd in the end to leave all veils behind.

The purpose of life is that of emancipating stars. It is we who condone substitutes and accept approximations for realities.

XLII

DOMINE JESU CHRISTE

In things above, as in things below, when the King is thought to be dead, our cry should be: Long live the King!

Eucharistica

Poor, foolish penitent, whose streaming eyes
See Christus dead in agony, He lives;
Take comfort; He comes down into thy heart:
Thou hast received Him in thy sacrament!

Beyond the symbol of the old beliefs stretch the great fields of faith.

XLIII

DOMINE, NON SUM DIGNUS

But the prince in banishment is not less the royal prince.

Misdirection

We have falter'd in the way that they directed
Who set us first to walk in the true way;
We have palter'd with the truth which they expected
We should set so high before us,
And the banners that are o'er us
Are the ensigns of a nation gone astray.

This notwithstanding, all roads lead to the spiritual Rome, though the true path is one.

XLIV

ITE, MISSA EST

It does not really signify that the way is long, if it is that which leads home.

Stars of Empire

From East to West the soul her journey takes,
At many bitter founts her fever slakes,
  Halts at strange taverns by the way to feast,
Resumes her load and painful progress makes
  Back to the East.

Many travels and many metamorphoses may still remain, both within and without the long chronicles of vanity. It is only by a title of limitation that the Mass is ever finished.

XLV

THE SECOND GOSPEL

Undeclared

Wisdom with its trumpet word
In a myriad volumes heard;
All which unto love belongs
Chanted in uncounted songs,
Up and down the endless ages;
Things divine in sacred pages—
As the sands of the seashore—
Taught with tongues of gold of yore:—
When to-morrow is to-day,
What can still remain to say?
One thing look'd for—one unheard;
Only that unutter'd word,
Echoes of the sense of which
All our spoken words enrich,
And shall yet, with clarion call,
Alter and transmute them all.

It is for this reason that literature is itself a mystery, operated by the convention of instituted rites.

XLVI

DEO GRATIAS

There is drought and there is weariness; but so long as we go forward, it is well.

Gratias Agimus

For the glory which now is over and the star which
has passed away,
We thank Thee, our Lord! It is night,
And the place of Thy peace is the place of a perfect
light;
But here in the depth of the darkness, as there on
the shining height,
We thank Thee for night and for day.

Et nox sicut dies illuminabitur.

THE POOR BROTHER'S MASS-BOOK

XLVII

A VALEDICTORY ASPIRATION

Let us pray, in fine, for those truly sacred offices which are not in reality conferred by any right of succession, but do at times impose themselves.

Of Priestcraft

Could God have given me my desire,
  Or if God would grant it now and here
One boon, I wot,
Should wreathe my lot
  As the star is wreathed by a fire—
  Fair aim, high purpose, but far, I fear!

I would put my making of songs aside—
  Vain strife to utter what can't be said;
And it should be mine
The bread and wine,
  By mighty mass-words deified,
  To change in substance from wine and bread.

And then in some lonely fane apart,
  Or—little matters—in crowded street,
With a soul contrite,
From altar's height
  I would nourish the empty heart
  With hidden manna and angels' meat.

That which has hinder'd me hinders yet,
  Though the higher part of faith is mine ;
'Tis the gift to know
That here below,
  Fair as the blazon'd signs are set
  They shadow only the things divine.

Holy and grand though the Church may be,
  The types it mixes with things foreshewn,
And a place denies
To the too keen eyes
  Which past the mundane types can see,
  And, symbols past, to the truth unknown.

Yet may I hope, is it over bold ?—
  Somehow—somewhere—it shall come to pass,
While I still live,
That my King shall give
  To me, like Lancelot, Knight of old,
  Grace, and a twelvemonth to sing my Mass.

PART IV

THE BOOK OF THE KING'S DOLE AND CHANTRY FOR PLAIN SONG

THE BOOK OF THE KING'S DOLE

THE PROEM TO THE KING'S DOLE

THE blessed legends tell that God made man
After the fashion of the cosmic plan,
And hence, in miniature and outline, he
Holds all its vastness sacramentally,
Being its mirror and its synthesis.
Nature's great elements are therefore his,
To high perfection in his frame refined
And in pure motions of the natural mind.
Thereto was added, far exceeding sense,
A certain rare and secret quintessence—
By those well known which seek the Holy Place
And the light shining from the Father's face.
Thereby man's natural and human part—
With all the fire of mind and fire of heart—
Did suffer transmutation and receive
The gifts from God of those who well believe.
Hence such high pathways of the soul he trod
As are reserved to those who walk with God
And joyful in the mystic city dwell:
All this at least the sacred legends tell.
But in some way which passes mortal thought
Man's royal nature unto shame was brought;
Whence that which once was elemental fire,
But held thereafter the divine desire;

And that which being virgin earth of old
Was quintessentially transform'd to gold;
Such strange corrosion underwent and loss
That angel gold was turn'd to dragon's dross,
While the immaculate and virgin earth
Was turn'd to common clay, of meanest worth.
O, image of the One! What evil spell
Could thus prevail, the sacred legends tell.

Behold him now, from early place and state
Sent into exile; there, disconsolate;
There, lame and halt and blind; there, inly maim'd,
Within a desert Nature unreclaim'd
Set, as he could, amidst all toil and pain,
His unprotected body to sustain
And his poor wounded soul to soothe and heal!
O, voice of ages, raised in wild appeal!
Must man for ever in such dolour dwell?
Ah, list again what sacred legends tell!

For on the straits and sorrows of the soul
There came the balm and mercy of the Dole.
Yes, the King's Dole from the King's Place was sent
To soothe and strengthen in our languishment,
And thus were some through many ages fed
With wine transmuted and an alter'd bread,
By faithful ministers distributed,
And in the blessed chantry of the King
Set up for service high. The censers swing

There, while for ever the great altar rays
Burn in the darkness of our mortal days;
And, 'midst the sick humanities, do there
The white-alb'd ministers, with tender care,
Pass and repass, repeating words of peace—
O'er cups that fail not in their fair increase
And the unfailing host's white miracle,
Strong to sustain, to save—as legends tell.

And so the soul of man, amidst the waste,
Of its first nourishment can dimly taste,
Whereof the saving virtue works within
Against the venom of the life of sin;
The age-long hurts within the soul are cured,
The blind eyes open'd, the old heights assured,
And though without the Chantry, through the waste,
Of death in place of life still exiles taste,
The blessed shrine abides for those who seek.

With loving aspect, mortified and meek,
Still in the reverence of the rites concur
Each solemn voiced, slow moving minister;
The bread is broken and the wine is pour'd,
The broken spirit is to health restored;
And, wash'd from stain, the travel-weary feet
Are fairly rested by the mercy-seat;
Then, through the open door which stands behind
The altar, passing, they go forth and find
That hidden house whereof the legends tell
In words of rumour, words of oracle.

THE BOOK OF THE KING'S DOLE

THE PEOPLE OF THE MYSTERY

Soror Janua Cœli	*High Priestess of the Sanctuary*
Pater Omnipotens	*Pontifex Maximus*
Frater Filius Redemptor	*Priest of the Order of Melchisedec*
Pater Servus Servorum	*The Great Abbot of the Chantry*
Soror Beata Pulchra	*A Stained Virgin*
The Loving Father Christian Rosy Cross	*Doorkeeper*
The Little Soror Puella	*A Child of the Mystery*
Frater e Millibus vix unum	*Most Wise Sovereign and Epopt*

The Familiars of the Holy Office: the Commemorating Chorus of the Faithful, id est, *Hierophants.*

The Scene of this Greater Initiation is the assumed Sanctuary of the Holy Assembly, with the Veil of the Holy of Holies behind the Altar.

THE BOOK OF THE KING'S DOLE

THE CEREMONY OF OPENING THE CHANTRY

THE Convention of the Holy Assembly takes place mystically in the Sanctuary of the outward Church, and there is no Temple, having a *Locus Sanctorum* and an abiding Presence, in which the Rite of the King's Dole cannot be appropriately worked. The particular arrangement of the Holy Place is shewn in the Faithful Words of the Mystery, and it is so simple that any cathedral and at need any hermitage, with the necessary issue behind, can be appropriated as a hold for the pageant. It should be observed, or at least in most cases, that the Sanctuary is not oriented according to the cardinal points, because the East follows the Master. The entrance at the imputed West of the Chancel is guarded by two Great Pillars, inscribed, in the tongue of men and angels, with the respective words MERCY and SEVERITY. The broad intervening space is taken up by the five steps of the chancel, but ingress is not attained, except at need by the Epopts, through the Rood-Screen betwixt the Pillars, as the column inscribed SEVERITY is the Place of Indulgence by which admission is given from without.

At the imputed East behind the Altar there is a heavy curtain embroidered with figures of palm-trees. A certain natural light filters through the Chantry, but it is tinged and transmuted by intermediaries of coloured glass and by emblazonments in the great windows North and South, belonging to the body of the Church. An enormous TAU Cross lies upon the Chancel steps, but there is no figure of man extended thereon. The Lamp of the Sanctuary, which burns at the opening with exceeding brightness, and the major lights of the Altar illuminate the place moderately.

The Most High SOROR JANUA CŒLI, the Most Merciful PATER OMNIPOTENS and the Released FRATER FILIUS REDEMPTOR enter the Sanctuary from the curtain behind the Altar. They are followed by the Chorus of Hierophants, which pours in through a secret door opened on the eastern side from within the Pillar of Mercy. These are types of a great multitude which no man can number. Lastly, the FAMILIARS or SERVANTS OF THE HOLY OFFICE enter through a similar door opened in the Pillar of Severity. There is a crowd of worshippers in the body of the Church; these are Postulants, external Servitors, and Probationers of the Lesser Grades, who follow the Stations of the Cross, tell the beads of the Rosary, or recite orisons at the side chapels in aisles and transepts, where the ordinary services and public offices are conducted, seemingly with no one seeing or understanding what takes place in the Sanctuary. The Loving Father CHRISTIAN ROSY CROSS is seated within the door of the Rood-Screen looking down the great nave.

The General Assembly in the Chancel having repaired to their proper places, the SOROR JANUA CŒLI, officiating as Celebrant-in-chief, commences the Ritual of the Mass with the *Introibo ad Altare Dei*, as in the Ordinary of the Missal, the two *Pontifices Maximi* assuming the functions of Deacons. The Liturgy is in outward respects identical with the authorised form, but there are certain changes in the Epistle and Gospel parts, while the Preface, the Canon, and the Secreta seem entirely different. The words of Consecration are unknown, but it is supposed that these also are the formulæ of a more secret Rite. After the *Panem cœlestem accipiam*, the office for the time being is altogether suspended. The Celebrants turn towards the body of the Chancel, the SOROR JANUA CŒLI having her back to the Tabernacle, the PATER OMNIPOTENS, as First Deacon, being on the Gospel side of the second Altar-step, and the FRATER FILIUS REDEMPTOR at the Epistle horn of the third or lowest step.

THE BOOK OF THE KING'S DOLE

SOROR JANUA CŒLI

With recollection, in the Name and Cause
Of all which stands behind the written laws
And is the last intention of the word
That even here is by no Epopt heard,
I witness to the city and the world
How Grace abounding has all flags unfurl'd,
Prompting me here and now to exercise
That gift of ministry which in me lies
And to decree forthwith a sacred thing:
This venerable chancel's opening,
So to dispense the King's most Royal Dole
And to enrich thereby the chosen soul.
But heedful first that all be duly done,
With sacred names is this true Rite begun;
Some ye shall utter in your hearts, but most
Praise clearly Father, Son and Holy Ghost.

PATER OMNIPOTENS

We know, High Sister, these are One in Three,
Saving the Hallows and the Mystery.

SOROR JANUA CŒLI

What sacred usage to the Rite is brought?

PATER OMNIPOTENS

The reservation of illumined thought.

STRANGE HOUSES OF SLEEP

SOROR JANUA CŒLI

And what does reverence of reserve impart
To this high formula of secret art?

PATER OMNIPOTENS

That sacramental numbers can enfold
The truth which never is by numbers told.

SOROR JANUA CŒLI

The sense hereof expound with loving word.

PATER OMNIPOTENS

They that have ears to hear long since have heard.

SOROR JANUA CŒLI

The power within me your reluctance presses.

PATER OMNIPOTENS

The truth I hold to all high truth confesses,
But let the lesser issues cease to vex:
De minimis non curat sacra lex.

SOROR JANUA CŒLI

Does truth more dimly shine in less than great?

THE BOOK OF THE KING'S DOLE

Pater Omnipotens

It is the measure of all high estate,
Yet does the ample mode the less contain;
And hence the wise commend us first to gain
All that which signifies and leave the rest.
What is the end by which a man is blest?
What exile fell upon him far behind,
Suspending faculties, beclouding mind,
Replacing royal heritage by want
And sealing memory's all-holding font?
How shall man now into his rights return?
Shall he the witness of his senses spurn,
The needs of flesh deny, and thus work back?
Or is there haply some more holy track,
Some gospel fitted to the words of joy,
Commission'd to fulfil and not destroy,
Telling that paths of rapture can be trod
And that beatitude leads best to God?

Soror Janua Cœli

Who, faithful and holy Father, answers these
Recurring questions of the soul's misease?

Pater Omnipotens

They who possess and can apply the keys.
Wherefore this hallow'd chantry, from the first
Of things, to quench the hunger and the thirst

Which spurs all seekers on, both quick and dead,
Was founded that the chosen might be led;
And into truth, as great evolved from less,
Or archetype declared in semblances,
Through many ages has it brought the race
First to the Blazon'd Veil and then the Face.

SOROR JANUA CŒLI

Ah, highest substitute of long-lost Word!
When moving spheres first sang together heard
And since not utter'd under any sky,
We in these precincts keep thy memory
And do, with licence full, dispense at need
Doctrine which is not life, yet holds life's seed;
We have a charter, out of storms and wreck
To pilot home from havens false afar:
Declare by what keen light of lambent star,
Priest of the order of Melchisedec!

FRATER FILIUS REDEMPTOR

One truth, one way, one passage and one term;
One grace of life which does in these confirm;
One sanative for worn and weary eyes;
One final and effective sacrifice!

SOROR JANUA CŒLI

To offer this and so dispense the Dole,
Accomplishing the raising of a soul,

Is here our great intent; for that we come
From places more withdrawn, where other some,
Call'd forth in turn upon a perfect track,
Our offices fulfil till we go back.

PATER OMNIPOTENS

And since the time is short, while needs increase,
With decent haste confer the dole of peace!

FRATER FILIUS REDEMPTOR

The grapes are heavy on the vines we tend,
The craftsmen few to make our harvest's end;
For lack thereof perchance we yet must go
And seek by public ways and green hedge-row.

SOROR JANUA CŒLI

Assist me, Brothers of the secret hidden!

PATER OMNIPOTENS

We should be with thee in the task unbidden.

SOROR JANUA CŒLI

And in accordance with the ancient rule,
Let us confess the purpose of our school!

STRANGE HOUSES OF SLEEP

THE SYMBOL

We do by knowledge testify and hold
One sainted plan, high-wrought in days of old,
Set in these precincts forth and duly kept.
Here, while humanity at large has slept,
The Dole has gather'd from all peopled tracts
Cleansed hearts adjusted to exalted acts,
And takes them softly to this place apart
For one great work of science and of art,
Whereof we here divine the whole intent
As deeply fix'd in spheres of sacrament.

SOROR JANUA CŒLI

So, therefore, Brothers, in the Light's great Name
And in the heart of heart remembering,
Beyond all spheres which do their place proclaim,
The one asylum which the rays enring
But cannot enter, let us freely ask
The virtue needful for so great a task !

FRATER FILIUS REDEMPTOR

High light, as ever, on our labour falls ;
Beyond its manifested beams there calls
The still small voice, which unexpounded is,
From formless, hidden and obscure abyss.

SOROR JANUA CŒLI

What first behoves the Keepers of the Dole ?

THE BOOK OF THE KING'S DOLE

FRATER FILIUS REDEMPTOR

To watch over the safety of the soul,
Lest out of time and mind the work should pass
And where the reverence of recipients was,
For dearth of penitents prepared and those
Who seek the altar bread, some deep repose,
By portal side, which knocking never stirs,
Should fall at length upon the ministers.

PATER OMNIPOTENS

Mistress and queen, the soul is guarded well;
Even in pools of sense still works our spell,
As on the heights where comes awakening
And those which stand for stars together sing.

SOROR JANUA CŒLI

What time is reckon'd in the world without?

PATER OMNIPOTENS

Dawn, and the watchers of the morning shout!

FRATER FILIUS REDEMPTOR

All times are ours who do the call obey,
Prepared with sacraments both night and day.

STRANGE HOUSES OF SLEEP

Soror Janua Cœli

Prayer as of old, or act of prayer, beseems,
At least in memory of former dreams,
What time by rites the heart in sleep was stirr'd
And life in tokens was administer'd.

PRAYER AT OPENING

The dawn of high rites comes like morning's dawn :
Be therefore with us from Thy seat withdrawn !
No homage hither unto Thee we bring,
Nor blessing ask who live beneath Thy wing
And do Thy substituted lights reflect.
Thou wilt not fail to lead and to direct,
While fair success shall crown our holy zeal
Who neither seek arcana to reveal,
Except with licence in salvation's pale,
Nor to withhold what can in quest avail
The dedicated heart of chosen man.
Success still follow on the age-long plan,
Which, after deep, condition'd, long research,
Gives entrance firstly to the inward church
And doth, unfailing at the times of need,
The outward church unseen but surely lead
By ways of exile, far as woes attend,
Through inhibitions which by turns suspend,
That all who at the Temple's porch begin
From step to step may climb and enter in !

All powers benign which here are strong to save,
Send past baptismal font, up sounding nave,

First at the chantry steps to kneel in prayer
And then the sanctuary's secret dare,
That by the highest altar's holy shroud
They may find egress from the field of cloud,
Nor wholly fail who have in fine recourse
Sole unto Thee who art their primal source;
But through the fire of cloud to light of fire
And past all fires of light find their desire;
Wherefore the praise is Thine and surely given:
May all high crowns be theirs; crown Thou in
  Heaven! [*A pause.*

SOROR JANUA CŒLI

All power within the outward Church I lift
Beyond these vestured regions of the mind,
Beyond the rays which pierce through gulf and rift,
The veils beyond, into the Church behind;
That so when term is more with font allied
And lesser issues are construed aside,
The weaker vessels visible to eye
May serve the office of our mystery.
Brothers, we here complete a sacred thing,
Which is the function of our opening!
In the great Name and in the Name beyond
That greatness, whereunto all stars respond,
And by the power within me vested here,
I open widely these great gates: Draw near!
The treasures of the Dole are offer'd free:
Let all thereto entitled come and see!

[*Here ends the Ceremony of Opening the Chantry.*

THE RITUAL OF THE LIFTING OF THE VEIL

The First Observance, or Twilight of the Gods

The Celebrants face the Altar. The two Deacons form a half-circle with the High Priestess, who takes the Chalice from the Altar and lifts it on high.

Soror Janua Cœli

Exalted Fratres, justified, anneal'd—
Behold the Treasure of the Dole unseal'd!

Pater Omnipotens

Here is the food of man, from every eye
Conceal'd by veils until the man shall die.

Frater Filius Redemptor

I see the children's bread transform'd to meat,
Whereof the Angels in the Presence eat.

Soror Janua Cœli

The place beyond the Holy Place has sent
Its messengers—on what high purpose bent?

The outward chancel in the outward gloom—
Say for what end we here and now assume
Into the place apart since time began,
And yet assuredly the house of man?

FRATER FILIUS REDEMPTOR

One further step to take the great command
Decreed since epochs immemorial,
Beyond all offices of heart and hand,
That, since the chosen follow on the call,
It may at length be possible to tell
How fully has the indefectible,
Perpetual end been joyously fulfill'd,
Thirst quench'd and longing in attainment still'd.

The Most High SOROR JANUA CŒLI gives the pontifical blessing with two fingers lifted and again turns to the Altar.

SOROR JANUA CŒLI

The earthly elements are taken up
From sacrificial paten and from cup,
That things which here are visible, made clean,
May be exalted by the things unseen.
We therefore recognise the type and sign,
With all the terms and veils of things divine,
And whatsoever in its order known
Has the great mystery signified, has shewn

Forth before man the hidden essences
Which to extract he toils with weary stress.
But with much worship, for the rest, herein
We do remove them also and begin
To cleave alone unto the second sense,
As to confess the third, with all which thence
Takes forward souls, from earthly bonds set free
And temporal measures of eternity.
To such an end, by operative art
Presenting pictures from the world's deep heart,
We will forthwith this grade administer:
Rites beyond rites arise: who hold, confer.
These grave reflections warn, for our behoof,
Not from old signs and rites to stand aloof:
Now let us therefore here of bread partake
And here with wine our thirst symbolic slake.

At this point the Ordinary of the Mass is resumed, subject to the Proper of the Chantry, for the communication of the High Priestess and Deacons in accordance with the Secret Liturgy. The Ordinary is again suspended subsequently, and what then follows in the Rite takes place between the Communion and the First Oblation.

SOROR JANUA CŒLI

We are not worthy in Thy House, O Lord,
To enter: cleanse us by Thy Holy word!

At the hands of the Celebrant-in-chief the PATER OMNIPOTENS communicates in both kinds, with bowed head, kneeling at the Gospel side of the highest Altar step.

THE BOOK OF THE KING'S DOLE

Soror Janua Cœli

We are not worthy here Thy gifts to set:
Do Thou in clemency our faults forget!

The Frater Filius Redemptor communicates, at the hands of the Celebrant, in both kinds with uplifted face and high extended arms, kneeling on the Epistle side at the second Altar step. The High Soror Janua Cœli replaces the chalice and paten containing the Hosts on the Altar, at the southern side of which she then kneels in adoration. The Little Soror Puella, who is Rosa Mystica, a Novice of the Order, comes forward in white robes from the side of the Pillar of Severity and ascends the steps of the Altar, with the forms and genuflections prescribed in the Rubric. She lifts up the paten, turning towards the Celebrant-in-chief.

Soror Puella

The body of God defend me!

The High Soror communicates in the element of bread. The Soror Puella replaces the paten, exalts the chalice and again turns towards the Celebrant.

Soror Puella

The blood of God expend me!

The High Soror communicates in the element of wine. The Soror Puella replaces the chalice on the Altar, and turns with extended arms towards the body of the chancel.

SOROR PUELLA

The life of life in our Sustainer end me!

She returns as she came. The High SOROR remains kneeling and prays in a subdued voice as follows:—

SOROR JANUA CŒLI

O not because we hope in Thee, our Goal,
Do Thou from formless centre draw us on,
Nor only since upon Thy help the soul
Hangs utterly whose course, so long begun,
Draws in the chancel of the King's High Dole
Some distance towards a semblance of the end!
But seeing that both term and end art Thou
And we came forth from Thee long since, extend
Thine efficacious help to those who now
Feel, while we near Thee, as the days succeed,
An infinite extension of our need!

PATER OMNIPOTENS

There is no grace in charity, no love
Of man and man which of itself can reach,
By any ways, the height of things above,
Till that descends which us alone can teach
With silent eloquence and golden speech.

FRATER FILIUS REDEMPTOR

Ah, uncreated glory, ah, infinite
White world of the irradiate still light!

Worlds to the Crown, but still a world above:
All fonts and springs and wells are those of love!

The Deacons rise; they descend the steps of the Altar and face it on the Epistle and Gospel sides. Soror Janua Cœli *also rises and turns towards them.*

Soror Janua Cœli

If any novice, who has watch'd his arms
And overstay'd the night with its alarms,
Stands at the postern and is meet to see
What lies beyond all common chivalry,
Let now the open'd postern take him through!
If any Master past his chair of state
Discerns the splendour of a further gate,
Impearl'd beyond the still void and the blue,
That gate may open when he stands outside.
If any consecrated priest appointed
To humble ministries of outward cure,
Seeks other oils than those which first anointed,
For him the chrismal treasures of the Dole
Are open'd, like the arms of mercy, wide
To work the ordination of his soul.
The aperture, though straiten'd, shall be sure,
And still at end thereof new rites allure.

A silvery bell rings softly within the Pillar of Mercy; the door of ingress opens; a neophyte bearing the bells enters within the Chancel; he is succeeded by the partisans of the Sanctuary, some of whom carry seven-branched candlesticks, and by one who swings a lighted thurible. The Candidate for advancement, who is termed FRATER E MILLIBUS VIX UNUM, follows in the vestment of a white friar, having the tonsure of the order on his head, which is also encircled by a faint nimbus. Scarlet crosses are embroidered before and behind on his habit, and he wears a large ring of profession on his right hand, with which he makes the sign of concealed doctrine in front of him. The Loving Father CHRISTIAN ROSY CROSS, as the Warden of the Gate, joins him on the left side, carrying a great white stone, in the form of a cube, on a cushion. The air also gives up the SOROR BEATA PULCHRA at the right of the Candidate, bearing a basket of cut flowers for strewing. The Familiars of the Holy Office place the seats of the Celebrants before the Altar, over against the lowermost step thereof. As the procession passes up the Chancel, the officiating Pontiffs take their seats, with the High SOROR JANUA CŒLI forming the centre of the triad. At the same moment a large Host rises from the chalice on the Altar and shines with transforming light. The High Abbot of the Chantry comes forward with jewelled mitre and golden crook. The acolytes and servers part on either side as FRATER E MILLIBUS VIX UNUM approaches the Abbot, before whom he stops with crossed arms. The Sponsors of the Candidate pause behind him.

PATER SERVUS SERVORUM

Whom lead you hither?

THE LOVING FATHER

One who not in vain
Is Epopt call'd and Most Wise Sovereign.
He, having first as Postulant been brought,
Was seal'd with sacraments and after taught

Effectively and well, till, in good time,
He graduated for the mundane clime
And sweetly enter'd into perfect sleep.
There, haunted long by imagery deep,
Wild wings he beat against the ivory gate
And striving ever towards the waking state,
Some secret doctrines in the twilight dim
Of life's strange houses were proclaim'd to him,
As unto one who half, ere morning, sees
High semblances of lesser mysteries
And takes refreshment of false wine and bread.
Thereat illumin'd and discomforted,
As many seekers have before him found,
He learn'd that those aspiring to be crown'd
Already taste the death of earthly joys
And find life's treasures are the children's toys.
So thence it came to pass that, human love
Taught to renounce because such heights above
Offer'd their summits through the mist, he knew,
At least by legends high, of unions true
And took therein a further secret grade.
Thus time and circumstance the groundwork laid,
By lights which in succession fade and fail,
Of some fantastic broideries of the veil,
And Nature sanctified was set aside.
Far reaching ministries, which deep and wide
Forth spread their missions, at the first were tried
And full of delectation in their place
Allow'd, but wanting the exalted grace;

Wherefore the Candidate was thus made free
Of the high service of a fourth degree.
So was he left, as one would think, alone—
Say, with the dreams which haunted him, unknown
Suggestions of the something which subtends
All that is here discern'd, which somewhere ends
In the great term of God, yet does not give
Meanwhile sufficient food for souls to live.
Therefore the Epopt who has since attain'd,
By certain secret magnets still constrain'd,
Did more consistently aspire, and trod
The paths which by convention lead to God.
These towards the very centre and the core
May actually trend, for many roads,
Straight or circuitous, in fine restore
True hearts inflamed to high desire's abodes;
They in a sense which Epopts understand
Are temporary centres close at hand
And great preparing grades, till circumstance
Shew forth the true path for the soul's advance.
Thus was the Candidate supremely taught
And through external channels safely brought,
With certain tinctured glasses of the mind,
To gather something of the light behind
And yet another mystery to pass,
Touching the most high sacring of the Mass.
In moving pageants first the Rite appeal'd,
Some quests, some meanings of the Graal reveal'd;
And then unfolded to his earnest search
In part the office of the outward Church.

That Church did therefore to his heart disclose
The many petals of the secret rose
And underneath the vastness of their screening
A tinctured heart of the more hidden meaning.
Therein the restless soul, to gain its end,
Does the high treasures of its force expend.
Out of the dim allusions and mere hints
It strikes, in mystic night, the saving glints,
So that beyond the dark it dimly sees
Penumbral gleams and hallowing mysteries.
The signs and portents of the light which lifts
Its beacons past the variable rifts,
By work of secret winds, were thus laid bare,
As pathways giving on the clearer air.
So taught the soul itself and so was taught;
Thus on the matter of the work it wrought,
Through all purgations, the refiner's art,
Transform'd and perfected from grade to grade.
The substituted maxims which depart
From all convention's ways, the lines new laid,
Unto high semblances of doctrine led.
Hence it is meet and right and just that such,
Being perchance exalted overmuch
By great subsidiary names, should now
Take higher pledges and adventure how
From mystic death are raised, in fine, the dead.
As sponsor of the Epopts, upon whom
Devolves such task, about their whole estate
I certify, before they pass the gate,
Having once made unto myself a tomb,

Within the auspice of another sun,
As analogue and compend of the One.
Therefore, by all that has been proved, of loss
And gain, advancement, carriage of the Cross,
I do proclaim this Sovereign Prince has shewn
His title-deeds for entrance to his own
And call on those who here the Dole dispense
To grant him quittance for departure hence.

Soror Janua Cœli

Most loving Father, your commands, disguised
As meek petition, shall in order due
Our notice gain who, otherwise apprised,
Hold in remembrance the memorial true
Of this beloved Epopt and most wise
Prince of the Royal Secret, held from eyes
Profane among the Archives of the Gate.
And when the final values here we take
A fitting end we deem that he will make
Of his protracted visionary course,
Scaling some further height to reach his source.
Unto this end, with adjuration fair,
Prithee, commend him to the Abbot's care;
Then, crossing once again the chancel's floor,
Resume your place behind the secret door,
Since other candidates perchance await
Admission, seeing that the hour is late
And that the ends of all the age are near.

THE BOOK OF THE KING'S DOLE

The Loving Father

Into the holy hands of Mother Church
I place the issues of my time-long search
And all the Postulants of grace far brought,
So to be judged and pardon'd, raised and taught.

The Loving Father Christian Rosy Cross gives the sign-in-chief of the Chantry and returns to the South-West, where he stands in the angle of the Rood-Screen, between the door thereof and the door in the Pillar of Mercy. The Soror Beata Pulchra mingles with the Familiars of the Holy Office in the Northern part of the Hall and passes for the time being out of sight.

Soror Janua Cœli

Frater e Millibus vix unum, long
Straining your ears to catch the marriage song,
Come forward; set apart all human fear:
Place in the Abbot's hand your own!

The Pater Servus Servorum leads the Candidate towards the East.

Soror Janua Cœli

In mine
The ancient guardians of the Bread and Wine
Receive you:

The right hand of the Candidate is placed by the Great Abbot in that of the Chief Celebrant.

SOROR JANUA CŒLI

And do welcome and make free.
Your pledges and disownments, sworn of old
At each symbolic grade and high degree
Of your advancement, in our rolls we hold:
Do you renew them freely here and now,
With mind prepared to take a final vow?

THE CANDIDATE

Prove me, O Steward of the things of type
Which here begin to fall as fruit o'er ripe!
My pledges have been kept, but higher lead
I follow now and, as it seems, proceed
Thither, whence first I came, long ages since,
Beyond the offices of priest and prince.
These obligations from the soul dissolve
And other orders other bonds evolve;
Whence I look rather that my faithful pledges
Should, in the final ordeal, by the edges
Of my precipitous path stand round to-day,
Keep me equilibrated in the way
And save me at this last from the abyss.
For now, meseems, I come where great death is,
And seeing that so long, through bad and good,
I have sustain'd my cross as best I could,
Full time it grows my cross should carry me.
No less, if other vows than these must be,

Before the bitterness of death can pass,
I hold myself to consecrate once more
This militant church which veils what once I was
Before I seek in faith the further shore.

The Celebrants rise and form a circle about the Candidate with the Great Abbot of the Chantry, who stands a little to the left behind him.

SOROR JANUA CŒLI

The great asylums none shall need seek out,
For they descend and him are built about,
And so the further shore is closer far
Than any hands which we can stretch forth are;
But that firm faith to which your heart responds
Declare, and comfort us, in place of bonds.

THE CANDIDATE

(*With bowed head.*) I do recite my fix'd adhesion
first
To all those sacred symbols which the thirst
Of human nature illustrate to reach
Things which exceed the limit of our speech.
I call on God to witness I receive
Their import full and do in them believe,
Saving the solemn clauses of the art
Conceal'd, by which the greater truths impart
And do at need interpret lesser things.

Wherefore, before the Unity made known
In mortal ways by Trinity alone,
One God in Persons Three, I claim to make
Confession, and the Chantry pledges take;
Unto which task my soul the title brings
That, howsoe'er in ways of sense I slept,
All ancient secrets of the Dole were kept
From common knowledge ever in my heart.
Whether made known at secret shrines apart,
Where the great rites are work'd, or half divined
By inward ways untaught, the same were shrined
In depths of thought which speech has never stirr'd,
Lest I should lose the hope of the True Word.

Further, I do confess that Nature's voice
Did first in saving ways my soul rejoice;
But when the hour arrived to reach her term,
At the dividing ways, I can affirm
That I put by her ministries, with mind
To great elections call'd, and so resign'd.
I do acknowledge with express intent
How far the outward Church my soul's ascent
Prepared and did exhibit; if at last
Beyond such ministries advanced I past,
I have not ceased at need to own her claim,
But have extoll'd her Holy Place and Name,
And also in the night of dream's eclipse
Maintain'd her truth and mission with my lips.
Hence if I go this day through death to wide
Horizons, let it be as fortified,

At least in thought, with her last rites, that so
The plain believer shall not come to know
Aught for his strength unmeet—that other way
Some souls tread, *mortis in examine.*

Lastly, with full conviction and complete
Assurance that the Angels' mystic meat
Is more than broken bread, derived to man
By hallows of the sacramental plan,
I do affirm that he who entrance wins
Into the Church's conscious life, begins
Clearly to see that through the wider gate
No tittle of the work is abrogate
And that, however far proceeds the search,
All high assemblies still remain the Church.
That apex where the seraphs' songs are sung
Is but the mystic ladder's furthest rung,
And at the base thereof, where children stand,
The hand that guides is still the self-same hand:
To all which subject, here I set aside
The outward sign for what is signified.

While the Confession is recited the Familiars of the Holy Office remove the seats of the Celebrants to the South side of the Chantry. When the Candidate has made an end, the circle is broken up; the High Priestess and Deacons turn towards the Altar and the procession passes to the steps, at the first of which the High Priestess again faces the Candidate, from whom, by the direction of the Great Abbot, she receives homage on his knees and communicates in return her benediction, which is given with open hand, to indicate that between her and him the veils are withdrawn by his reception.

Soror Janua Cœli

We do maintain the signs with steadfastness
Because their shadows in some part express,
Some part convey, the grace from hidden wells,
Being conventions and yet vehicles.
We also know that in the soul's release
And happy entrance to the paths of peace,
Far must she pass along the secret roads
Before she leaves all sacramental modes;
Yet in the end set free, she goeth thence
And so attains direct experience,
Even fruition of a perfect joy—
Which to promote, these rites all powers deploy.

The Great Abbot

Not as a pledge of faith but as a sign
That well and worthily the Law Divine
Which calls on those with knowledge to conceal
Until the law for each shall break the seal,
And in due turn each come to understand;
You will upon the consecrated hand
Of this High Priestess print the sealing kiss
And so in peace depart where deep peace is.

The Great Abbot bends slightly the head of the Candidate, who is still on his knees, and the latter kisses reverently the hand of the Soror Janua Cœli, who at the same moment stoops forward and gives him the *Osculum Fraternitatis* on his forehead, saying:—

THE BOOK OF THE KING'S DOLE

SOROR JANUA CŒLI

The service of my hands I take, and give
Lip service, that in death you yet may live.

The Great Abbot raises the Candidate and places him with his back to the Altar, facing the concourse of witnesses.

THE GREAT ABBOT

FRATER E MILLIBUS VIX UNUM, Prince
Of the most Royal Secret, Sovereign
Most Wise, by these and other titles—since
Those who in mysteries their advance attain
Must put aside both titles and degrees—
Fulfil your final duties unto these
Who here their lesson in the prudent path
Put well to heart and whom the silence hath
In holy keeping!

The Candidate still faces westward and certain insignia, not otherwise specified in the Rubrics, are removed from beneath his Vestments.

THE CANDIDATE

Brothers of the Veil,
The honourable tokens of the road
By which my soul has travell'd, thus I set
Before you, knowing that you need them not,
To count among the hallows of this spot,
Or work perchance some further service yet
Among the places where the great lights fail.

Let other postulants in order wear
These high insignia, turn'd as light as air
To us on threshold of the true abode,
And as before the presence of the King!
Here at this last pause made upon the wing,
In native poverty, my leave I take
Of whatsoever, for the mystery's sake,
Has been held precious in the outward ways.
May God his faithful of the nave and aisle
Raise to the chancel in a little while
And on the hidden secrets let them gaze;
May those who stand without the sacred fold,
Versed in the ways of folly and of sin,
Receive the call before their right is sold
And knock and find it open and come in!

The acolytes extinguish their torches. The three Pontiffs ascend the steps of the Altar. The SOROR JANUA CŒLI raises the chalice from the Altar and, with the exalted Deacons on either side, turns round, displaying the sacred vessel with the Host shining above it. At the same moment the Great Abbot of the Chantry turns the Candidate, so that the light of the Elements falls upon his face. He then directs him to kneel upon the lowermost Altar step. The procession approaches with extinguished torches and smoking censer. The only light of the Chancel is now that of the Sacred Elements. There is a great hush of silence, in which the still air suddenly becomes very cold. The SOROR BEATA PULCHRA moves a little distance towards the centre of the Chancel, and the flowers die in her basket. The Loving Father CHRISTIAN ROSY CROSS takes his place in the due South, carrying the Cubic Stone, which he opens without speaking. The cube unfolds as a Cross, which he exalts, and about the four branches the words MORS JANUA VITÆ flicker like writing on a wall. The bells of the Chantry begin to toll slowly and with a muffled sound. The procession disperses. The SOROR JANUA CŒLI descends the steps of the Altar, with the Elements exalted before her. On the Host there can be discovered very faintly the imprint of a Slain Lamb, in place of the canonical *Sigillum.*

SOROR JANUA CŒLI

The sting is sharp; its victory is brought
To nothing; common faculties of thought
Through dissolution pass and are not found.
Here is inflicted the deep, orbic wound
Which does not fall on tissues and on nerves—
Unerring work of hand which never swerves,
Striking within, beyond the place of sleep,
To open ways through which a soul may sweep,
Past all earth's surging waters unanneal'd,
And the old war-cries past, where peace is seal'd.

O Lord, too long upon the exile's leave
Sent forth, we are not worthy to receive
Thee in our house, nor stand in Thine, but Thou
Hast come among us to instruct us how
Some need divine impels Thee to fulfil
In our respect Thy high, most holy will!
By many names we did of old invoke
And seek Thine aid, but there was one unknown,
Through which at length we come into our own,
In truth, as sleepers from their swoon awoke:
By that great title undeclared we do
In fine receive Thee, and with homage true.

The High SOROR JANUA CŒLI lifts the Host, from which no splendour now emanates, over the bowed head of the Candidate.

SOROR JANUA CŒLI

Behold the Lamb of God, in sign again,
As from the ages and foundation, slain!

The High Priestess breaks the Element of bread over the chalice. The Communicant raises his head, about which the nimbus radiates more brightly, and receives the sacrament after the ordinary manner of a layman. When he has communicated in the one kind, the chalice is also administered, with the words:—

SOROR JANUA CŒLI

By this most holy unction and the great
Divine Compassion, at the open gate
To postulants exhibited, may those
Who are the wardens and that gate unclose,
Shew forth the path which out of Mercy leads
To Understanding, as a broad, still sea,
And thence in Wisdom's further deep recedes;
So may its issue at the end for thee
Not in the Kingdom but the Diadem be!

THE CANDIDATE

In Thy strong hands I do, my God, commend
My spirit, utterly attain'd this end.

[*The* CANDIDATE *falls back dead.*

THE BOOK OF THE KING'S DOLE

The Familiars of the Holy Office

May this man's soul, and all whose souls with his
Are join'd by faith, attain that rest which is
Reserved unmanifest in worlds to come!

The Hierophants

Strong men in chariots and in horses some,
But we in the Lord's name invoke and bring,
To ease our needs, a votive offering.
Hear us, O Lord, invoking: Save the King!

The Great Abbot

The wounded bird is saved upon the wing
With those whom death has spared: Long live
the King!

THE SECOND OBSERVANCE

The Obscure Night of the Gods

A veil is thrown over the Candidate and he is laid upon a funeral litter. The Chancel is now entirely in darkness, except for the flame of incense fuming in the thurible of the acolyte. The Familiars of the Holy Office move silently over the floor and place the candles of the dead about the catafalque. The Familiars light the candles, but they give only uncertain and flickering rays, making the darkness visible. The High SOROR JANUA CŒLI has ascended the Altar steps and replaced the Sacred Elements. The Deacons minister about her, and the ablutions are performed as usual. Certain propers of the faithful departed are added subsequently in a low voice, but their purport is not distinguishable. Subsequently, the High SOROR turns with extended arms, saying:—

SOROR JANUA CŒLI

The Lord be with you, Fratres: it is well;
The grace long ask'd for falls on Israel!

THE HIEROPHANTS (*with muffled voices*)

And on thy spirit, as of old it fell.

SOROR JANUA CŒLI

Peace also, spiritual sleep, bereft
Of sounds; all secrets in the Kingdom heard

Are utter'd ; nothing is for mystæ left
Except the word behind the spoken word.

She descends from the Altar, which she faces with the Deacons on either side.

SOROR JANUA CŒLI

My fault, my fault and my most grievous fault!
So long as savour rests in earthly salt,
I do repent this drag-net for the skies
Brings so few offerings for the service wise.

The High Priestess and Deacons prostrate themselves on the steps of the Altar, as at the opening of the Mass of the Presanctified. They move, on rising, in silence to their chairs in the South, and sit with hands laid palms downward on their knees. They remain in this attitude during the whole ceremony of the Candidate's raising, except for the share which they take in the burial service.

The SOROR BEATA PULCHRA moves forward from the northern side of the Chancel, scattering her dead leaves and withered blossoms.

SOROR BEATA PULCHRA

Friends, who have known me and whom still I
know,
Through each vicissitude of voided ends
And passage forth from show to greater show,
With all the calls that friends can make on
friends—

Look at me, say what woe is like my woe!
Does not my legend's true memorial
Bear better witness than the purple pall
Can ever bear that those who lie beneath
Are folded closely in the arms of death?
And as the shroud about a maiden's head
Is mournful evidence that one is dead
Who was most fair and little stain'd, we trust;
So do all legends which my loss recount
Praise that which issued from the primal fount
And was so free and beautiful and pure
That virgin earth had little kin with dust.
But the woe came and woe must still endure,
Though not indeed was mine the conscious fault,
Fierce war's most bitter fortune, in the vault
Now peopled by the planetary ghosts,
As by mute substitutes of former hosts.
Thus on me uninvoked there fell the curse
Which work'd the shipwreck of the universe;
Angels and men were both involved therein,
As by æonian strife where none could win.
So that which first came forth inviolate
Through bright creation's newly open'd gate,
Suffer'd a ruthless sacrifice and fell
Within the circle of the dreary spell
Which time served solely further to confirm,
Starving all knowledge of its final term.

She approaches the head of the bier and scatters wither'd blooms upon the veil which covers the Candidate.

THE BOOK OF THE KING'S DOLE

Soror Beata Pulchra

As one who leaves another in his need
Farthest and most extreme, thy soul indeed
Has issued, the last act of life which pass'd
'Neath other spells than I have ever cast,
For life itself divided thee from me
Than common stroke of death more utterly.
Thou wast not mine therein, and here it seems
That, coming out from all the power of dreams
And all my range exceeding, thou hast brought
Thy daring course from crowded realms of thought,
By ways unknown, to tenebræ of gloom,
And dost in death itself o'erreach the tomb.
In doubt I gaze where thou art here intern'd
Lest intervening portents undiscern'd
Should manifest more dubious semblances
Than are the obvious limits of life's stress,
Strangely to counterfeit the mortal breath.
Truly thou art not mine in life or death.
I give thee back to those of whom thou art,
Since in this place I have no power nor part,
Though here my sacramental doom must bring
Me, for some mystic work of witnessing.
Such witness faithful, full of vows, I bear
That all my claims on thee who liest there,
If not fulfill'd, at least extinguish'd are:
The cup has pass'd from me; I raise no bar.

I, the great spirit of the world, to this
World's prince unwillingly awhile allied,
Since that must hold which here my hindrance is
From restitution, who was sanctified,
Do thee renounce and thee therein give back.
Tempests remain and tarries tardy peace,
Nor tidings come from ends where labours cease;
But thou returnest on thy starry track.

The SOROR BEATA PULCHRA, having emptied her floral basket about the catafalque, is escorted by the procession, carrying extinguished torches and an unswung censer, on her departure from the Chancel through the door in the Pillar of Severity. She pauses in her exit, turns to the East by South, and in place of the secret and invariable signs of the Chantry, she gives the Sign of the Cross extended, with uplifted arms. The High SOROR rises from her chair and says aloud:—

SOROR JANUA CŒLI

Where is the light which on the path is shed?

PUELLA

(*From the western end of the Chancel*).

The light is quench'd, most High, the man is dead.

SOROR JANUA CŒLI

Are his accusers present?

PUELLA

He has earn'd
His quittance, and the charges are return'd
To those who did the schedule first prefer.
Mark'd: No advice—wherein all grades concur.

SOROR JANUA CŒLI

Then, recollected, we in short proceed
To the high office in such case decreed.

The Thurifer approaches with censer, which he presents on his knees. The High SOROR receives it; the Deacons rise and take the ends of her cope. She passes to the East of the catafalque, which she circumambulates, following the sun, and the incense fumes over the veil with aromatic fragrance. The circumambulation being completed, the Pontiffs pause in a semicircle at some distance from the bier in the East. The Great Abbot of the Chantry comes before them with an extinguisher, circumambulates, following the sun, and puts out the lights successively, the one light in the East being excepted, using the following formulæ:—

PATER SERVUS SERVORUM

At the First Light—

The Light of Life, the light of outward things,
The semblance of the Kingdom and its Kings.

At the Second Light—

The basis of the first fantastic gleam
Which falls on Israel in the tide of dream.

At the Third Light—

The shadow of the ray reflected down
Which lifts the earthly towards the heavenly
town.

At the Fourth Light—

The flush of conquest when the gloom reveals
The first libation of the cup which heals.

At the Fifth Light—

The middle splendour of the light derived
To all four points upon the man arrived
From the great deeps, carrying certain keys
Which are his title to the high degrees.

At the Sixth Light—

The Light of rigour where the glooms begin
To manifest the path which works within,
By far devolving ways and heights uptending,
For those who keep the virtue of ascending
As others keep well-ruled an inward fire.

At the Seventh Light—

The Light which fashions first the great desire
To see the temple, palaces and halls
Which those receive who follow the great calls,
And build the house that is not made with hands,
Giving on certain solitary lands
And shores, for ever to a silent sea
Confessing an unsearchable mystery.

He approaches the Eighth Light, which is slightly outside the rectilineal line formed in the oblong square by the other funereal candles.

At the Eighth Light—

The Light which shews the gates of the great deep,
That lifts its voices in the dark and sings
Of correspondence in the higher things:
The gates which prophet and strong leader saw
But could not promulgate their secret law,
Whereby the hidden matters, and the rest
Behind the faculties of reason, keep
Some larger issues past the reach of sleep
And in all common vision unexpress'd.

The Bells of the Chantry again toll with a muffled sound. The Great Abbot of the Chantry raises the Eighth Candlestick and carries it, slightly exalted, by the South-East, behind the Altar.

STRANGE HOUSES OF SLEEP

Soror Janua Cœli

And blessed are the dead whose souls go forth
Beyond the darkness of the mystic North
To reach the source wherein all light increased
Resumes its higher splendours in the East:
Henceforth and ever from their labours these
Share in the Centre's still activities.

Pater Omnipotens

Beneath the realm of internecine strife,
The length of days and endless years of life.

Frater Filius Redemptor

The Resurrection and the life am I:
He that in me believeth, though on earth
He may be dead, shall live and cannot die,
And I will raise him to the second birth.

The tenebræ alarm is heard behind the Altar, and the Eighth Light is exalted at the same moment in the high shrine placed over the Tabernacle.

Chorus of Hierophants

Ye who are laden, come: the Master saith;
I hold the keys of Hades and of Death!

THE BOOK OF THE KING'S DOLE

THE FAMILIARS OF THE HOLY OFFICE

O grave! where is thy victory; and where,
O death! thy sting?

[*A long pause.*

SOROR PUELLA

(*Speaking from the western end of the Chancel*)

The man enshrouded there
Has lain three mystic days.

THE LOVING FATHER

(*Speaking from the angle of the Rood-Screen*)

The worms are swarth;
The cerements close.

PATER SERVUS SERVORUM

And still he is not dead.

FRATER FILIUS REDEMPTOR

He has slept long and dreams have visited.

PATER OMNIPOTENS

Time grows to waken.

THE THIRD OBSERVANCE

The Raising in Darkness.

SOROR JANUA CŒLI

LAZARUS, COME FORTH!

The Candlestick on the Altar is removed from its place. An unknown hand is raised over it, as it is drawn down slowly, and extinguishes the light, after which it is placed behind the Altar. The Chancel is thus in complete darkness, the thurible being also closed down, though it continues to give forth smoke at intervals. The Great Abbot approaches the catafalque and puts back the veil from the face of the Candidate, who begins to speak.

THE CANDIDATE

He who through frozen deeps alone has been
And where the great gods are, their glories seen
Doth seek no longer after length of days,
Seats of the mighty, or the choric praise
Which up and down the mystic chancel pants
In fires and salvoes of the hierophants.
But grasping what abysses intervene
And what suspensions of the vital law
Obtain, from Aleph in the heights to Tau,
One great experiment of him lays hold—
Who once, he knows not how, his birthright sold—

The secret ways to follow, where they trend
From Tau to Aleph, and attain his end.
These having found and being fain to start,
But knowing also that the goal is far,
I rise at call, preparing to depart
And take all thrones, ascending towards my star.
Assist me, brethren, who so far am led :
Lo, I am he that liveth and was dead !
[*The Candidate rises in shadow.*

Prayer of the Hierophants

The road is open and if ways are long,
The guide who inly operates is strong,
And thine own soul, which takes thee, shall not fail
Once and for all the Crown, in fine, to hail.
Thou dost not call for angels, nor hast need
Of outward mentors to assume the lead,
While every step upon the forward track
Shall render it the harder to go back.
And yet the workings of the ancient curse,
More secret than the serpent's wiles, reverse
All human judgments ; so there lives not one
Beneath the common splendours of the sun,
Or in the hidden lights of those whose course
Is lifted high to reach their primal source,
That ever heard of office or of grade
Wherein the subtle virus is, in fine,

Expended utterly. Thou hast therefore said
Farewell to sleep, and dreams for thee are quench'd ;
An age-long vigil is hereafter thine,
By frozen zones of dreadful glory blench'd
And destitute of all but one resource,
Which is exhibited, through inward force,
Most patiently to that not less within
Conjoin'd, that torrent inexhaustible
Which, when the floodgates of the soul begin
To open, in the soul's abysmal well
Pours, till the soul is vivified and fed
And the last rite is so consummated.

We pray thee, therefore, coming thus from trance,
Be vigilant, be wary in advance ;
And to the great conferring Powers, which do
All the rough edges of the sleep worlds hew
That whom God calls may unto God be led,
We also pray incessantly ; may true
Help be derived at need—and now to you !

Pater Servus Servorum

Within the bosom of the mystery
Raised in the darkness, ere the Rite of High
Observance raises into limpid light,
He who has come thus far, with one last veil
Behind the hallows of all holy things—
The bells, pomegranates and tall palms—in sight,

By semblance here is taught ere semblance fail;
And for the last time call'd by mystic names;
While the great epopt circle him enrings
Once and for all, and then the past is past.

Shall there be need to say, with such degrees
Received, that all the common smoke and flames
Of outward life are shadow'd and o'ercast
With portent lights? In spite of narrow grooves,
The deeper meaning round the slighter moves;
Wherefore the child upon his mother's knees
Is by the hauntings of the Holy Word
Pursued, has sacraments administer'd.
Thou too in paths of novices hast trod
And long been offer'd bread and wine for God,
But shalt henceforth, by this advance of thine,
Receive Eternal God for bread and wine.
God's body then was taken to thine own,
Now must thy soul into His Soul pass on;
Wherefore thy part in earth its term attains
And former things are left for greater gains.

The Candidate

As one far-travell'd, and withal outworn,
Or one in a new planet newly born,
The higher ministries of health I need:
Give me to eat and drink—strong meat indeed!

THE FOURTH OBSERVANCE

The Candidate is instituted in Light

A great light begins to glow through the embroidered veil behind the Altar. The Loving Father CHRISTIAN ROSY CROSS advances to the centre of the Chancel. The Familiars of the Holy Office marshal at the Northern side and file out. The Hierophants at the southern end follow. The Acolytes with thurible and extinguished torches go last, the SOROR PUELLA escorting Father ROSY CROSS. The illumination of the Chancel continues. It becomes in this manner a Chamber of the Presence. The Candidate, who has knelt on the lowest step of the Altar, is raised in solemn form by the High SOROR JANUA CŒLI, and this raising in the Light is performed without words. The Great Abbot of the Chantry, assisted by the two Deacons, escorts the High Priestess to her throne in the South, and the Candidate is then taken by the Deacons only to the Sacrarium-in-ordinary of the Chancel, where he removes his monastic habit and is clothed in pontifical vestments, as if for the celebration of High Mass. When all is ready the bell of the Sacrarium is rung, and the three Priests come into the Chancel, ascending the Altar steps, as at the point after the Communication of the Faithful. But in place of the Post-Communion the High Priestess rises and, still standing in the South, says:—

SOROR JANUA CŒLI

The Lord is with us and with thy spirit too,
The which henceforth by ministration true
Shall be pour'd out from its unfailing fount,
Directing others still in gloom of dream

To their awaking and the further scheme
Which gathers man into the Holy Mount.
This is thy Compline service, to the night
Farewell, and institution in the light,
Which, that the city and world may know thy fame,
By power within me vested, I proclaim.

The High SOROR resumes her throne. The two Deacons descend the Altar steps, make the Ritual Genuflection, and resume their seats on either side of the Celebrant-in-Chief. The Candidate is thus left standing alone, with his back to the Tabernacle.

THE CANDIDATE

Most faithful witnesses were heard of old
Who in the Kingdom took their stand and told
How the withdrawn, invisible King abode
Beyond all gates of knowledge; and the road
By which his secret palace must be sought,
In sacramental speech, they also taught.
Dark is the Kingdom, though cloud-breaking rifts
Open at times, what welkins and what lifts
Exhibiting, as if through ivory gates,
And dreams thereof, reality awaits!

But closing spells and semblances collect
Full soon, to dim the paths and misdirect
The seeker, since the Kingdom, on a day
Far and how far, put from the Crown away,
Has sat in exile and the folds of sense.
But many Powers successively upraised

Have intervened because of man's defence,
So he from certain altitudes has gazed
On many secrets of the world's advance;
But still there rests conceal'd the countenance
And royal beauty of the King, from sight
Shrouded in glory of the limitless light.
The world's whole hope is in the paths which rise
Through spheres successive, by which first the Crown
Transmits benignant influences down,
As sacred wine is pour'd from sacred cup,
To heal the Kingdom; and whereby the wise
Do from the Kingdom to the Crown go up.
Those paths are steep; therein the weary halt—
Fail, as it seems, and, utterly at fault,
Do find in darken'd houses doubtful rest.
Yet are those paths left open and the quest,
By him who has been worthily prepared,
Not for rejection in the end is dared.
He, after length of labour and of stress,
Shall pass from tumult into silentness,
From which no voice on peak uplifted high
Has ever come but once to testify.
Now therefore in the road from star to star,
By great election having come so far
And being pledged to follow on the call,
Through power within me vested, once for all
I do my Chantry office here begin
And by these presents have myself read in.
I know what Virtues from what veils behind
My ways have watch'd and have my path assign'd,

Who also on the reverence of high search
Wait to make known, beyond the outward Church,
The Great Assembly's work which leads unseen.
But having so been taught and thus made clean,
The soul, once guided, with the guiding hand
Is here made one, and that enlighten'd band
Has join'd which doth from stage to further stage
Assume the Church, and every closing age
Seal with a certain sign of progress won.

Dear friends, when Rites and Liturgies are done
And the anointed celebrants have gone,
Signs in the heart remain to lead men on.
So, ere I go, I pray you, join with me
For one point more in this our Mystery;
Then shall the Chancel be restored with peace
Unto the Church External, to increase,
We trust, the graces and the favours kept
For those who long the faithful sleep have slept,
Yet have preserved their sanctity in dreams
And certain hauntings of diviner schemes,
Through all the witnesses of sense, have own'd:
May they too wake and be in light enthroned!

If aught is left unfinish'd, I beseech
That my deficiency, atoned in each
Of you, my peers, may be so well fulfill'd
That more of good shall follow than we will'd.
If one of those to whom I once belong'd,
Rightly or not, regard himself as wrong'd

By me, his free forgiveness here I crave,
And may he have good issue from his grave !
If, when the earthly things aside I put,
One creditor unwittingly I shut
Out of his honourable share, I trust
To have his quittance now, and all star-dust
I will exchange for stars and so atone
When he and I shall come into our own.

My mystic titles having placed aside,
That less no longer may from great divide,
At times perchance their memories shall stir
Faint odours of sweet spikenard and of myrrh,
And in the outward worshippers' suspense
Increase the savour of strong frankincense.

The Candidate descends the steps of the Altar, and the Celebrants rise as he passes by the South-East side.

SOROR JANUA CŒLI

We are but signs which faintly here express
Some accents of remote, uplifted things
Beyond all speech : do thou at parting bless !

The Candidate gives the benediction with a triple Tau traced by his pastoral crook.

THE CANDIDATE

Be healing ever in thy holy wings!
The sign evoked from the great sea art thou;
Deep Understanding in the Chancel now
For ever dwells with thee. And those who take
The great diaconate and semblance make
Of lesser office, are the tokens here
Of emanations to the Crown more near,
Three, by intention one, and one in three:
Last sign dissolving towards reality.
In veils like this we almost see the dawn—
Bear witness still: I am the sign withdrawn!

The Celebrants resume their seats and the Candidate, with a new light in his nimbus, passes behind the Altar, opens the veil of the Mysteries and enters within. The veil closes behind him and through it the radiance of the First Resurrection pours with power and glory. There is a brief space of silence, and after this the Candidate speaks very softly and slowly from behind the veil, that is to say, in the Chantry which is over against the Sanctuary of the Militant Church, being of it but not in it.

THE CANDIDATE

The root of roots and basis of foundations,
The place of prudence which the wise alone
Approach, and ever in their labours own!
This, after Orders, Choirs and Dominations,
Leads, and can only lead, to the most high
Knowledge of the divine priority.

Deep Understanding is it named as well;
The advocate whose potent sweetness stands
Twixt God and man with high uplifted hands;
The Sabbath and the rest of those that dwell
Within the higher peace of Israel.
From outward zones hereof the influx falls,
From star to star, through palaces and halls,
And he that knows—or in at least such part
As ever enters the created heart—
These deeps, discerns the well of generations
And how the soul, unclothed and lightly shod,
Through human sonship leaps to that of God.
So is it, standing by this limpid sea,
What orient from on high to seek I know,
When to the realm of unvoiced mystery,
Deep beyond deep of wisdom, forth I go.

[*A pause.*

I do proclaim that there are many heights,
Whereof the first alone the Fathers trod;
I see beyond the still depths other lights,
With ways of entrance to the maze of God.
The soul, not utterly from symbols freed,
E'en in these holy places, knows indeed
At once the grace behind the sacrament
Fair overshadowing the outward sign,
And something more behind it, which has lent
The dim allusion of more high intent,
Like after savour of imperial wine;

THE BOOK OF THE KING'S DOLE

As if within illuminating blaze
Of visible, superinceding rays,
The soul were inwardly advised to mark
Some greater wonder centred in the dark.

The High Soror Janua Cœli, assisted by the Deacons of the Rite, proceeds to the High Altar. The Acolytes with kindled thurible and lighted torches enter, followed by the Familiars of the Holy Office and the cohort of Hierophants. The Rite is resumed in the Office of the Ordinary of the Mass. The Ablutions are performed, and after the *Dominus vobiscum*, the *Placeat tibi*, proper to Masses for the Dead, is recited in secret, with the variations peculiar to the Chancel. The usual Benediction is followed by the Second Gospel, which is given rapidly, so that the text is not readily distinguishable. After the *Deo Gratias*, the closing of the King's Dole is taken in solemn form.

THE HIGH OFFICE OF CLOSING THE KING'S CHANTRY

The Soror Janua Cœli faces the Western end of the Chancel from the Altar. The Deacons do likewise from the Epistle and Gospel sides, standing respectively on the third and second steps. The Secret Signs of the Holy Assembly are given with the particular variations attributed to each office of the Celebrants, and are followed by the collective sign common to all members, and now repeated by all.

Soror Janua Cœli

Brethren, we know the mortal life of man
By one incredible divorce began
Which did the bridegroom from the destined
    bride
For all the calculable times divide;
But restitution shall be made at last,
Old rights restored and all suspensions past:
Unto which term, that loyal hearts attend,
This holy grade we bring to hallow'd end.

Pater Omnipotens

Take these last words at parting from a soul
Drench'd with all light conceived: The greater
    goal
Lies infinitely far, and farther still

Beyond the dream that we can shape is He,
Without distinctions born of thee and me:
He can alone us satisfy and fill.
O primal last and immemorial first,
We have put on perfection and our sin
Have set aside, yet end as we begin,
A-hunger'd and unquenchably athirst!
What is thy union but delighted pain?
We rest not even in Thee while we remain:
Give us that greater marriage that will leave
Neither the soul which toils nor hands that weave,
To compass Thy true end, nor Thy will work—
The signs of self in such abysses lurk:
Take back Thy plenitude and us take back,
Leaving of all we were nor sound nor rack!

Soror Janua Cœli

If any brother, by the Altar's call,
To serve entitled and assume his stall,
Is of his rights unwittingly bereft,
And hence is still among the semblance left;
We here proclaim our undivided will
To abrogate all ruling laws until
Each Son of Doctrine in his class shall gain
The end design'd, and none without remain
Whose strife is firstly to be purged from sin
And then exalted to the heights within;
While, for the rest, so far as work unseen
Can out of lesser goods lead man at large,

We stand behind them with oblations clean,
Nor length of ages shall outwear our charge.
We with our eyes have seen, our lips have known,
The soul has enter'd where the soul alone
Participates, and patience never sleeps.
We, who have reach'd the heights, do know the deeps
And out of many regions of the curse
Have risen to possess the universe;
So on the deeps we call, the lost therein,
Houses of profanation and of sin;
We stand with open hands, with bleeding hearts
By many sorrows pierced, and all our arts
Do exercise to rescue and redeem.
So out of nightmare and of torpid dream
Do we all orders of the world uplift,
Till all shall know the chancel and the gift;
For we have felt the chastening and the rod,
And through great sorrows have gone up to God,
To find that hell is God more deeply heal'd
And that beatitude is union seal'd.

Frater Filius Redemptor

The creeds and dogmas into silence fall;
They gave us many nothings who need the All.
So therefore solemnly, with reverent lips,
Out of our hands the sacred vessel slips;
The hosts are broken on the patens; Christ,
Who for all needs that we could voice sufficed,

As manifested God we worship low.
Beyond these outward ministries, we know
An inward passion and necessitous
Craving, which cannot be assuaged in us
Till we, who have been saved by Christ, shall fall
Beyond all rescue in the All of All.

Soror Janua Cœli

In the High Name which is not spoken here,
Where ministries of Names no more appear,
I close this Chapter of the Epopts brought,
By many doctrines in the Churches taught,
Unto the sacramental world's first term and verge,
Whence secret paths on other spheres emerge.
By these the soul must issue forth alone,
If ever it would truly reach its own.
Now are all rites completed; rites no more
Dispense the qualifying grace and give
The consecrations which prevail'd of yore:
The soul exalted learns alone to live,
Whence every pledge of him who gave I here
Without reserve into his hands restore,
That he who in the light of light is wise
May offer as he please his sacrifice
And those about him to their end bring near;
That souls which follow on the call of grace
Where signs and letters can no longer kill,
And look to stand at length as face to face,
May freely work the Dole's most holy will.

So therefore is the Order closed and all
Fulfill'd at present in this sacred Hall
In his regard who came through fire and cloud
To share those gifts herein to hearts allow'd.
Now it is finish'd—work of peace and sword—
And for the last time here we praise the Lord.

The High Soror Janua Cœli is led behind the Altar, and so into the divided veil, by the Eminent Pater Omnipotens and the Exempt Frater Filius Redemptor.

Pater Servus Servorum

(*Speaking from the centre of the Chancel*)

The Chantry back into the shade devolves;
The Dole, expended, fails; the Rite dissolves.

The Spokesman of the Hierophants

And with the surging backward of the things
External, let us to the King of Kings,
Once and again, accord official praise;
As saving help on the inferior ways,
Acknowledging the Lord of every Host—
The Triune, Father, Son and Holy Ghost.

The Foreman of the Holy Office

Most meet it is that priests of every clime
Sing Alleluia in the Paschal time!

THE SPOKESMAN OF THE HIEROPHANTS

Well done, thou faithful servant : enter in
Those nuptial joys which in the Lord begin !

THE FOREMAN OF THE HOLY OFFICE

We hold the Rosary, since beads began,
Most helpful to salvation of the man ;
We do commend to all by faith's rule led
The system of paid Masses for the dead ;
And we desire to see with one accord
The temporal power of the pope restored.

THE SPOKESMAN OF THE HIEROPHANTS

While for the Stations of the Cross we wait,
Let Christian Rosy Cross still keep the gate.

PATER SERVUS SERVORUM

So doth abysmal night on all descend :
This is the Chantry Mass-Book's very end.

The Acolytes lead the Procession. The Epopts file out through the Pillar of Mercy and the Familiars of the Holy Office through that of Severity. The Loving Father CHRISTIAN ROSY CROSS, in his capacity as Gate-Keeper, assumes the cloak and hood of a serving-friar. The Faithful crowd up and he sells to them scapulas and Agnus Dei tokens. The women of the crowd light votive tapers at tripods. Father Athanasius in the pulpit concludes the Sermon of the day.

FATHER ATHANASIUS

Therefore, my brethren, let not wiles delude;
So with this wholesome maxim I conclude:
Poor heretics may still be saved perchance,
But only by invincible ignorance;
And even so the camel, I testify,
Shall pass more easily through the needle's eye.

The Sacristans make the collection, and the organ opens the hymn: "GOD BLESS OUR POPE, THE GREAT, THE GOOD—" which is sung by the children with shrill voices.

FINIS

AT PASSING

AT PASSING

WHEN the day begins to break
    Call us back to life and light;
Leaving sweetly now we take—
                And so, good night!

Short or long we do not know,
    Dark at least the night-space seems;
Hearts are weary; leave it so,
                But kind be dreams!

Wish us thy good speed at end
    Who, committing all to thee—
Truest love and dearest friend—
                At rest would be.

And to keep us free from pain,
    With the eye's light in the eye,
Thus we pray thee: come again;
                Till then, good-bye!

Sense of all things slowly slips,
    Utter trust dissolves alarms—
Thus with lips against thy lips
                And arms in arms!

IN PREPARATION

The Hidden Church of the Holy Graal

ITS LEGENDS AND SYMBOLISM

REGARDED AS A MYSTERY OF INITIATION: ITS CONNECTION WITH OTHER MYSTERIES, AND A NEW THEORY OF ITS DEVELOPMENT

BY A. E. WAITE

PART I.—The Nature and Purposes of the Graal Quest, from the first institution of the Hallows to their ultimate removal.

PART II.—The Antecedents of the Legends in Folk-lore, showing that the elements brought over from this source lost their original character, and that a new tissue of symbolism was imported therein.

PART III.—The Implicits of the Quest concerning (*a*) the Secret Words of Consecration; (*b*) a Peculiar Apostolic Succession; and (*c*) an Ecclesiastical Pre-eminence following therefrom.

PART IV.—The Celtic Church, including Traditional Hereditary Keepers of Consecrated Objects, Vestiges of Concealed Words, Legends of Miraculous Altars, the History of Mass Chalices, and some particular forms of Symbolism.

Part V.—Mystic Aspects of the Graal Legend, embodying the Outlines of a Great Experiment followed by the Sacred Schools, and the Graal Legends re-expressed in the terms of this Experiment.

Part VI.—A Summary of Possible Interventions, being an account of several Schemes which are now voided, and the Analogies of certain co-existent Schools of Symbolism.

Part VII.—The Secret Church; the possibility of its perpetuation through the centuries from Apostolic Times put forward as a working hypothesis, including traces of a Process which differed from the Mind of the Church, but in the Mind of the Church only.

The Work is an attempt to set forth, after a new manner, the mystery enshrined in the old Romance Literature of the Holy Graal, and it has been undertaken as a consequence of certain first-hand considerations. The task has been imposed rather than sought out, and originates from a familiarity with analogical fields of symbolism, the correspondences of which must almost of necessity escape students who have not passed through the Schools of Secret Thought. The investigation is therefore designed primarily for those who have in some manner been connected with the Hidden Knowledge, and it will enable them to recognise affiliations which may otherwise be new to themselves. The full measure of the experiment is not reached till the final part, wherein the Graal Mystery is considered in its connection with the existence and survival of a Hidden Church.

Printed in the United States
104154LV00004B/10/A